Creative
Mexican
Cooking

Creative Mexican Cooking

★ RECIPES FROM ★
GREAT TEXAS CHEFS

ANNE LINDSAY GREER

★

TexasMonthlyPress

The recipe for Chile and Cilantro Pesto is adapted from *Cuisines of the American Southwest*, Cuisinart Cooking Club, Inc., Harper and Row. Recipes developed for the food processor are printed by permission of Cuisinart Cooking Club, Inc., © 1982 by Cuisinart Cooking Club, Inc.

Texas Monthly Press, Inc.
P.O. Box 1569
Austin, Texas 78767

   B   C   D   E   F   G H

Library of Congress Cataloging in Publication Data

Greer, Anne Lindsay.
   Creative Mexican cooking.

   Includes index.
   1. Cookery, Mexican. 2. Cooks—Texas. I. Title.
TX716.M4G74   1985   641.5972   84-24031
ISBN 0-932012-63-9

Book design by Helen McCarty
Photography by Kirk R. Tuck

Printed in Japan by Dai Nippon Printing Co. Ltd. through DNP (America), Inc.

To the greatest kids I know: my two sons, Don and Will, with love and enormous pride.

ACKNOWLEDGMENTS

Gratitude and affection to my tireless research assistant and dear friend, Judy Brenan, Carolyn Rice, who helped test and type and then test and type again, and my friends, both old and new, those innovative chefs and restaurateurs who generously gave of their time and talent.

TABLE OF CONTENTS

INTRODUCTION

"*T*ex-Mex" has become the popular catchall word to describe almost any food that has Mexican roots, ingredients, or presentation. If you want a clear definition, don't ask a Texan. He'll shrug his shoulders, give a puzzled look and an elusive answer. Give him a taste and all the confusion disappears. Despite the differences between the major cities—Austin, San Antonio, Houston, and Dallas—all Texas-style, Tex-Mex food is harmoniously linked to a wider world. Though Texans might not acknowledge it, this is just a piece of a much larger pie. New Mexico, Arizona, Southern California all have similar roots and a style of food that looks like Tex-Mex, sometimes tastes like Tex-Mex, and is often dubbed Tex-Mex. In the past, regional dishes had clear and well-defined differences; but with the rapid growth of the entire Southwest, particularly with the increasing number of restaurants specializing in native foods, these old guidelines are less obvious.

As Texas becomes more affluent, its culinary arts grow and change. So we see all over the state a new style of Mexican American food . . . a new Tex-Mex. Restaurant decor is moving from rather heavy, dark surroundings to a more "authentic" Continental or high-tech look. The traditional Tex-Mex "combination plate" of rice, beans, guacamole, and enchiladas remains, but there are more fresh fruits and vegetables, seafood dishes from the Yucatán, Continental cuisine from Mexico City, and an innovative Tex-Mex that combines local ingredients, a Mexican flair, and a fresh presentation. I visited hundreds of restaurants in Texas (in addition to New Mexico, Arizona, and California) in an attempt to find the movers and shakers of this new approach. While some places have an item or two that is unique, there are a handful of leaders . . . those who make a strong, personal statement and whose influence is seen throughout Texas.

Some of these innovators are chefs at Texas' most prestigious hotels, like the Loews Anatole in Dallas, the Mansion on Turtle Creek in Dallas, or La Mansión del Río in San Antonio. More often, they are dedicated restaurant owners and chefs who take risks and expend a tremendous amount of energy in their efforts to introduce a new atmosphere, new dishes, or a revival of classic Spanish or Mexican foods to a rather traditional Tex-Mex-oriented population. While not all Mexican or Mexican American, all are essentially self-made men and women . . . some motivated by hardships and the need to survive, others by a dream, and all by a love for their native foods and traditions. Their varied backgrounds are reflected in their food and the environment in which they choose to serve it. All take deep pride in their cuisine—all are eager to share their recipes, their knowledge, and their love for their craft.

As you read about these chefs and restaurateurs, you'll come to appreciate both their contributions and the cooking techniques that set them apart. As the popularity of our Southwestern food grows, many changes are still to come. A new, upscale, Southwestern cuisine is just now in its infancy. Small cafes like Cappy's and elegant restaurants like the Nana Grill, the Mansion on Turtle Creek, and Charley's 517 have their versions of this new cuisine. As American cuisine develops, its Southwestern and California expressions will continue to mix and grow—there is much to come.

Meanwhile, our selected few have been quietly paving the way. I think you will find their recipes and their personal stories interesting, inspiring, and illustrative of the pioneer spirit that makes Texas what it is.

Anne Lindsay Greer

Creative Mexican Cooking

Chefs and Restaurateurs

FONDA SAN MIGUEL
Upper Left: Coffee Toffee Pie
Upper Right: Almond Flan

Center: Pollo Pibil
Bottom Center: Fish in Garlic Sauce

CHEFS AND RESTAURATEURS

Bennie Ferrell Catering
Bennie Ferrell
Houston

Cafe Cancún
Ed Murph and Emilio Rodríguez
Dallas

Cappy's
Cappy Lawton
San Antonio

El Mirador
Mary Treviño
San Antonio

Ernesto's
Ernesto Torres
San Antonio

Fonda San Miguel
Mike Ravago
Austin

La Fogata
Jesse and Carmen Calvillo
San Antonio

La Hacienda
John Spice
San Antonio

Los Panchos
Araceli and Manuel Reyes
San Antonio

Los Tres Bobos
John Thorson
Austin

Mariano's
Mariano Martinez
Dallas

Mario's and Alberto's
Mario Leal
Dallas

Ninfa's
Ninfa Laurenzo
Houston

The Tavern
Ruben and Carmela López
Crystal City

Tila's
Clive Duval
Houston

La Esquina, Las Canarias
The Mansion on Turtle Creek

BENNIE FERRELL CATERING
Bennie Ferrell
Houston

When I was researching my *Cuisines of the American Southwest*, I spent six months tasting and testing tamales. The name Ferrell kept surfacing as creator of the most delicious tamales in Texas.

Mexican American, no—great cooks, yes!

In 1959, Bennie Ferrell began bartending for an early Houston caterer. Just before a party for one thousand people, Bennie's employer skipped town, leaving his employees and frantic customer floundering. Bennie came to the rescue and supervised the party preparations. The result: a huge success and the birth of a Houston tradition. As wife Norma remembers, "We didn't go into the catering business to make a lot of money, but because Houston needed good food and a dependable caterer."

The business started out in the Ferrells' home, where the garage was converted into a kitchen. The exigencies of congenial service and dependable food soon demanded a larger kitchen. Before long, the whole backyard was needed. Final expansion brought the Ferrells to their modern Spring Branch facilities, where the business can be found today . . . still outgrowing its kitchen while making hungry (and sometimes demanding) Houstonites happier.

The energy behind the business now comes from two Ferrell daughters, Cynthia and Peggy. However, mother Norma's love of cooking still brings her into the kitchen.

Says Norma, "My grandmother was a caterer in Mexia, Texas, although they probably didn't identify her as such. She had sixteen children, and because they were so poor, the only Christmas present the children got was a little cake, baked to order by Grandma. Another one of our grandfathers was a chef in a private home for a Houston oilman for twenty years. He has been cooking over forty-eight years, and no matter what he cooks, it's such a treat that you almost want to cry when you eat it. Our family came from Louisiana and Texas, and originally all our recipes were family recipes." The Ferrells cannot escape the Texas demand for Texas food—they've collected and created some delicious innovations seldom found in restaurants.

Peggy Ferrell sees their food as a combination of Louisiana French Creole and Texas country cooking. The Ferrells strive to serve simple, homecooked dishes in an artistically attractive way that pleases the eye as well as the palate. Their dishes have not gone unnoticed by other caterers . . . they have guided and inspired other caterers around the state.

CAFE CANCÚN
Ed Murph and Emilio Rodríguez
Dallas

milio Rodríguez had years of food training, Ed Murph supplied the club knowledge, and between the two of them they created the atmosphere and the style of food for a convivial meeting place as well as a fine-quality restaurant. Historically, the Tex-Mex "combination plate" evolved from a necessity to put nourishing food on the table quickly, at a reasonable cost. But Cafe Cancún has created an atmosphere which encourages people to linger. Ed and Emilio describe themselves as being in the people business. They wanted to provide a light and breezy place with a new style of Mexican food: "Tex-Mex could be found everywhere, but we wanted to offer something different, something light . . . Mexico City–inspired. We added live music, guitars, harps, or mariachis to provide a place where patrons could come in, relax, and spend the evening."

Interestingly enough, the food matches the environment . . . the salmon-colored walls, large windows, and polished wood floors project the ambience of a Continental cafe. The food takes on an almost Continental presentation. There are no fire-hot salsas or heavy Tex-Mex sauces but many vegetable dishes, salads, and simple, attractive presentations. Charcoal-broiled meats and fish are accompanied by vegetable quesadillas and fresh vegetables. Black beans, more popular in California than in Texas, are a Cafe Cancún trademark (California's affection for them is shared, I might add, by Dallas in general). The Corn Soup is simple, though unmatched.

A new atmosphere, attention to amenities, and a daring to lighten the food make Cafe Cancún an example many are following.

CAPPY'S

Cappy Lawton
San Antonio

Cappy Lawton may have been selected as one of fifty "Rising Stars" in Texas in 1982, but in San Antonio circles he is the epitome of a home-town boy who made good. A likable young businessman who began by designing airplane interiors, he has carved out a respected niche for himself in the restaurant business. His first restaurant, the Quarter Deck, only hinted at his love for the Mexican roots in Texas cuisine. Later, in Mama's Cafe, Mama's, and finally Cappy's, he served creative Mexican dishes alongside Tex-Mex and Texas favorites. Cappy's basic concept of serving good, nourishing food in un-usual settings has not changed. A devotee of the arts, Cappy looked to Texas architect O'Neil Ford and local artists to enhance the settings for his restau-rants—which range from Texas cafe memorabilia to a light and airy Mexico City look—and his food can be an eclectic creation or a masterful interpreta-tion of a dish from Mexico City.

A cook at heart, it's not unusual for Cappy to spend a sixteen-hour day super-vising his restaurants, then go home to create or perfect a dish for the daily blackboard specials. His love for native Texas food as well as for the foods of Mexico takes many expressions in his various restaurants. Cappy believes in people, appreciates the arts, and has a unique understanding of how to present food as an expression of the times. His restaurants are more than places to en-joy good food . . . they are meeting places. The atmosphere encourages you to stay . . . and the food makes you feel at home.

Cappy is devoted to serving fresh and healthful foods. He was the first to intro-duce grilled redfish to Texans, and he was one of several innovative restau-rateurs who created a Southwestern-style menu—part Mexican but not Tex-Mex, with new presentations of classic dishes from the vast Southwestern states. Cappy Lawton has become a leader in a creative expression of Mexican-inspired Texas food.

EL MIRADOR

Mary Treviño
San Antonio

Many of Mary Treviño's customers come hundreds of miles to enjoy her beautiful and delicious homemade soups. Mary has had recipes in *Bon Appétit*—and her dishes attract national food writers with sophisticated palates who patiently wait in line with her loyal clientele.

Mary's family originally came from Guanajuato in Central Mexico. "In Mexico, we learned to use what we had. Here we have very good meat, so you serve a good steak, a potato, and a salad. In Mexico we couldn't do that because we had meat that was not very good and a small amount of money." So Mary's family fixed soups and stews seasoned with imagination. All Mexican American cuisine has these simple, sensible roots, and the result can be a bland rice-and-bean stew or, as in Mary's case, an interesting soup that is as beautiful to look at as it is to eat.

Mary modestly calls herself an untrained cook. However, her passion for fresh herbs and other fresh ingredients and her adherence to classic techniques put both her soups and her restaurant in a class by themselves. *Bon Appétit* has praised Mary for her skillful techniques. If there is such a thing as a born cook, it is Mary.

"A typical middle-class Mexican breakfast would consist of foamy Mexican chocolate, fresh fruits, and bolillos. For dessert, my mother boiled tortilla strips in milk and sugar, an improvised dessert she called migas. For *meriendas*, afternoon parties, Mother fixed hot teas, such as lemongrass, cinnamon, or mint, and served crispy donuts, much like the beignets you get in San Francisco." Ingredients were often scarce and the food obviously simple—perhaps an inspiration to young Mary.

The day I visited her, she had just come from watching her son receive his doctoral degree from A&M, was operating the cash register, supervising the kitchen, soothing one of the cooks, and chatting with customers while I attempted to follow her through various soup preparations. Creative and unique, Mary's soup will distinguish her as a leader in the cuisine of Texas. True to her native Guanajuato, Mary too is known for her fine cuisine. Her soups are gourmet in the true sense . . . "good eating," artistically and lovingly assembled.

ERNESTO'S
Ernesto Torres
San Antonio

Ernesto is in the food business because he loves food. That's something most of us can readily understand, with gusto! He began as a waiter in the Grand Hotel in Monterrey, Mexico, then moved to San Antonio in 1961, where he worked at the Saint Anthony Hotel as a captain and as maitre d'hôtel.

Ernesto seized every opportunity to learn cooking techniques. One opportunity that has proven invaluable was his position at Handy Andy as assistant director under William Ardid, the gastronome in charge of food demonstrations. It was a natural step from his association with Ardid at Handy Andy to becoming maitre d'hôtel at Chez Ardid, one of San Antonio's finest Continental restaurants.

In 1981, Ernesto opened his own restaurant on West Avenue on the proverbial shoestring. His establishment seated only thirty-three, but he was supported by a loyal clientele who appreciated his Mexican-style seafood dishes, even if they did have to eat off paper plates with plastic forks.

Today Ernesto's has moved to a new, upscale location and has become one of San Antonio's fine restaurants. Its excellent food may cost more than fare at other San Antonio Mexican restaurants, but Ernesto's is always full. The restaurant is a family affair. Ernesto's wife, Grace, often supervises the kitchen. Daughter Belinda prepares some of the sauces and enjoys exercising her main interest, baking. Ernesto, Jr., when he is not cooking some French or Mexican specialty, helps out as a busboy.

The whole family takes pride in Ernesto's creations, particularly his butter sauces—an important contribution to the new wave of Mexican American Southwestern cuisine. These creamy sauces may contain crisp garlic or such classic Veracruz ingredients as olives, capers, and chiles. Made by the French *beurre blanc* method, Ernesto's sauces are rich—but the resulting dishes are surprisingly light. His green table salsa is unique, and his crabmeat crepes and nachos are being imitated in upscale Mexican American restaurants throughout the Southwest.

Ernesto is clearly a leader, an innovator, one whose contributions are becoming classics.

FONDA SAN MIGUEL
Mike Ravago
Austin

When you open the massive, imported wooden doors into the skylit Mexico City–style patio, it's like entering another world. The lush plants, the pigskin chairs from Mexico, and the inviting decor create an expectation of unusual dishes from the interior of Mexico. That's what Mike set out to do, and he won't disappoint you. An American with a Mexican mother, Mike has an inherent love for the native foods from interior Mexico and the Yucatán. His dream to bring these dishes to Texas began at Fonda San Angel in Houston, fifteen years ago. A student of Diana Kennedy's, he toured Mexico with her and spent thirteen years learning from her. Many of her dishes are served at San Miguel, though somewhat Americanized for Austin palates. Mike's experience as a cooking teacher enables him to run a consistent kitchen that often serves twelve hundred people on a Friday or Saturday evening.

Mike's dream has been to establish a replica of the Mexico City atmosphere . . . a setting for the food he loves and appreciates. His attention to skilled techniques and authentic ingredients is unequaled. Just as Diana Kennedy educated the world about the fine cuisines of Mexico, Mike is presenting an interpretation you can taste. He is unique in the state, keeping integrity in his dishes, giving credit to his well-respected teacher. This highly talented and modest young man has had the dedication and the skill to create an outstanding restaurant.

LA FOGATA

Jesse and Carmen Calvillo
San Antonio

*L*a Fogata is an excellent example of what happens when two backgrounds are successfully blended—the result is the birth of a San Antonio tradition at Jesse and Carmen Calvillo's popular restaurant. People are willing to stand in line, no matter what the weather or the hour, just to sample La Fogata's refreshing, innovative cuisine.

Jesse Calvillo came from San Miguel, a rural village in northern Mexico. Some of his earliest boyhood memories are of cooking outside over an open campfire, *la fogata*. "There was no electricity in rural Mexico, so, traditionally, nearly all the cooking was done out of doors. I can remember my grandmother making the tortillas by hand, cooking them with the meat and beans over an open fire on the ground. We were constantly cutting wood to keep *la fogata* burning." These boyhood memories started the dream that is now a reality.

Jesse's wife, Carmen, grew up in Mexico City, where her parents had been involved in the catering business for many years. Her mother started out with ten cooks, who prepared about five different plates each day and delivered them to customers throughout the city. Over the years, their reputation earned them one of the five most prestigious awards for excellent food in Mexico City.

When Jesse married Carmen, two distinctive styles of cooking as well as two backgrounds were joined. Carmen shared Jesse's dream to open a restaurant. Jesse credits Carmen's mother, who was an excellent cook, with being one of the major catalysts in making their dream become a reality.

"My mother-in-law was an idea person with follow-through. With her encouragement and help, Carmen and I hired one person and began our restaurant in a former Dairy Queen–gas station–hamburger drive-in." They renovated the building, striving for an attractive atmosphere, good food, and acceptable prices. The result is a charming, bright spot with plant-filled patios—almost a Continental-style cafe, definitely a radical departure from the typical Tex-Mex place.

Originally, the business served thirty to fifty people a day. Today, the Calvillos have managed to maintain high and consistent quality while serving up to eight hundred customers a day. Jesse doesn't have to rely on a manager; twenty years in the grocery business taught him how to buy good-quality produce. During working hours he is six people at once—flashing his good-natured smile to patrons, supervising his busy staff, and checking each plate for quality, consistency, and presentation. He has built a reputation on fresh ingredients, fresh handmade tortillas, and his and Carmen's unique interpretation of Mexican American cuisine.

Jesse says, "You eat first with your eyes." Perhaps the first to break away from a standard Tex-Mex plate, he pays great detail to presentation, keeping a simple integrity in each dish. People have come from all over the country, from writers for national food magazines and newspapers to curious fellow chefs, to discover La Fogata's secrets. Jesse and Carmen have continued to operate on one of their original premises: "Ideas work if you work."

And something is working at La Fogata. Jesse and Carmen are leaders in innovative presentation and a new, light interpretation of Mexican American food.

LA HACIENDA
John Spice
San Antonio

Just off a busy interstate highway, hidden amid a semitropical garden setting along Salado Creek, is a cluster of shops and restaurants called Los Patios, one of San Antonio's most attractive meeting places. John Spice's landscape business from Midland, Texas, has grown into a combined gift shop, restaurant, and landscape enterprise, occupying thirty-two acres along the creek.

John's first restaurant, the Gazebo, was constructed as a tearoom nestled around a patio. Hanging baskets and lush green plants soon made the Gazebo a popular attraction, rivaled only by the Brazier, a luncheon grill overlooking the creek. Los Patios' newest addition is La Hacienda, home of John Spice's unusual New Mexican–style dishes.

John researched restaurants and restaurant kitchens in New Mexico, Arizona, California, and even Mexico, testing and fine-tuning his recipes to suit San Antonio palates. His menu offers the classic dishes of New Mexico, spiced with his own creative touch. True to his restaurant profile, he buys his chiles fresh or fresh-frozen from New Mexico, thus maintaining the integrity of his dishes.

Although John says that his restaurants were not originally intended to be the main focus of the Los Patios compound, people are drawn to the pleasant parklike surroundings, the nursery, the fine boutiques, *and* the skillfully prepared food in the restaurants.

We think La Hacienda and John Spice are offering new and creative food, prepared with respect for its New Mexican origin and served with a distinctively artful presentation. John's salsas and his other innovative dishes will be adopted and adapted by others, but only here will you find authentic ingredients and techniques.

15

LOS PANCHOS
Araceli and Manuel Reyes
San Antonio

*A*raceli "Cheli" Reyes grew up in Mexico City, where she learned the restaurant business from her brother-in-law, "Pancho." Araceli wanted to share her love of Mexican foods, preparing all the dishes herself as she had learned them from her family. Los Panchitos, a modest place with about ten tables, was her first restaurant. Six years later, after a vacation visit to San Antonio, she encouraged her husband, Manuel, to expand their enterprise. The Mexico City restaurant was sold, and this brave new step resulted in the opening of Los Panchos in San Antonio.

The menu at Los Panchos changes continually as the family constantly aims at providing San Antonians with something different. Introducing an authentic combination of Spanish and Central Mexican cuisine to a Tex-Mex neighborhood takes a bit of pioneer spirit! Araceli describes her food as home cooking, typical of that found in the private homes of Mexico. For example, Los Panchos is one of the few places in San Antonio that serves the Mexico City favorites Carnitas and Cochinita Pibil Yucateca.

Cheli's brother-in-law comes frequently from Mexico to check on her Carnitas— and he's declared them to be the best he can find. During Christmas Cheli's customers will be treated to her family's version of a special Christmas chicken from her region. Her Chiles with Nut Sauce, a classic recipe from Mexico, is enjoying a new popularity . . . quite different from the more common chile relleno.

Los Panchos has been open only since 1982, but San Antonians are beginning to like the more exotic flavors that slip smoothly into its delicate sauces. Learning how to prepare something special for her customers and friends keeps the sparkle in Cheli's eyes. "What I enjoy almost as much as the cooking is to see someone's face light up with delight when something new tastes good. That is my real reward. I am always asking my customers what they like and trying to prepare things that appeal to them," she confides. And she always succeeds.

LOS TRES BOBOS

John Thorson
Austin

John Thorson, though anything but crazy, somehow earned the nickname along with two college friends. The friendship (and the name) stuck, and as a result their first restaurant was named Los Tres Bobos, the Three Crazies.

John was responsible for Los Tres Bobos's recipe development, which took him from Donna, Texas, to New Mexico for unusual recipes and fresh ingredients. Today, most of his sauces have a red or green chile base, usually fresh, whether they are made from California, Texas, or New Mexico peppers.

After the initial crash course in research and development, John began testing recipes by cooking for his partners and friends every weekend. Achieving consistency, considering the unpredictable nature of chiles, was a breathless challenge. John's goal was to introduce Austinites to something new and fun with universal taste appeal and local pizzazz!

The food at Los Tres Bobos combines California and New Mexico styles, tempered with Texas traditions. The dedication to fresh ingredients, fine-quality meats, and careful attention to preparation results in an unusual blend of innovative flavors, presented with John's attractive (and sometimes eclectic) style. But it works. And there's nothing very crazy about that.

MARIANO'S
Mariano Martínez
Dallas

Mariano Martínez started out in the restaurant business with an abundance of perseverance, faith, and enthusiasm and a shortage of education, connections, and cash. He did have the benefit of growing up in a restaurant family. His father started cooking in an early little cafe along the San Antonio River. Later, he opened a small place, El Caliente, which merged with El Chico (the training ground for many) and finally became his son's restaurant, Mariano's.

Reflecting on his parent's years in the restaurant business, Mariano says, "My father was an excellent cook. Cooks think in pictures, like chess players. They may not be able to remember data and follow the details of a recipe, but they have a feel for their craft and know instinctively when something looks right. Looking back, I can really appreciate my early investors, who had faith in me and those mental pictures of my projects and dreams."

Mariano feels that he has always been inspired by innovation, coupled with high quality. Like all the chefs and restaurateurs in this book, Mariano will not cut costs by substituting inferior meat or produce. He believes in the integrity of the fresh ingredients that he has used in all his restaurants. He was one of the first to offer a fine-quality homemade corn tortilla, though he is better known for his frozen margaritas, which he makes by a method now widely imitated in Dallas restaurants. Mariano's unique fajita, introduced in its San Antonio presentation, was new to Dallas. Nowhere else had I seen the gyro, a vertical barbecue combining several different kinds of meat, wrapped and then sliced off at the perfect moment to make tacos al pastor.

Many of Mariano's recipes have been developed by his family, his friends, or sometimes his well-known customers. An idea he credits to Craig Morton of the Dallas Cowboys became his famous Highland Park Nachos, spiced with the pickled vegetables from jalapeños *en escabeche*.

Mariano has taken many traditional favorites, some from other regions, then garnished them with his own magical and sometimes flamboyant touch. Like Ninfa Laurenzo, he has a gift for new and catchy names which help put those dishes on the culinary map. He has restored some of the mystery and romance to Mexican American food . . . a visit to Mariano's is a fiesta, and intentionally so.

With encouragement from his wife, Wanda, Mariano is looking toward the future, thinking about innovative ways to lighten food and promote its healthful aspects. If anyone can do it, this dashing, charismatic, and energetic young man can.

MARIO'S AND ALBERTO'S
Mario Leal
Dallas

Sitting in his elegant Dallas restaurant, with its peach-tinted walls, massive but tasteful Mexican portraits, plush carpeting, and generally opulent atmosphere, Mario Leal exudes enthusiasm. Mario left Linares, Mexico, in his teens to try his luck in the United States. His father kept encouraging him to return to Mexico, but Mario wanted to remain in the States and learn the restaurant business.

After early training with El Chico, Mario worked at El Mesón, a well-known restaurant in Mexico City. In 1972, he opened Chiquita's, his first restaurant. Not ever intending to serve Tex-Mex, Mario eventually found it necessary to satisfy his clientele. Chiquita's was a success—one of the first restaurants in Dallas to offer something new.

"I like to play around with new ideas in the kitchen and either create something or work with the chef to develop an idea. I get new ideas wherever I go. Even if I am at a Chinese restaurant, I may taste something and go home and try it on my family." Perhaps this is the reason for a new style of Mexican food all over Texas. It was certainly the reason for Mario's second restaurant, Mario's and Alberto's.

New dishes are often conceived by accident. Mario's Pollo de Crema "happened" when a cook dropped a few bits of chicken in the cream sauce slated for Chiles en Nogada. Another accidental acquisition came about when the kitchen was pressured by the arrival of unexpected guests. The shrimp, sliced improperly, ended up in a Shrimp Flauta. The Flautas Botanas Pipos were saved and named in honor of the unexpected guests, a culinary tradition.

Mario travels to Mexico for ideas, then returns home to fine-tune another creation. He claims that he is not a great chef—however, the quality of his food contradicts his modesty. Mario is imitated by many; his skills as a fine cook and his enthusiasm for new dishes make him a leader in his field.

NINFA'S
Ninfa Laurenzo
Houston

The incredible story of Ninfa's success sounds more like a public relations fantasy than the real-life struggle of Ninfa María Rodríguez, one of twelve children from Harlingen, Texas, in the Rio Grande Valley. In seven short years, Ninfa was able to woo Houstonians from basic Tex-Mex to a whole new style of food! Her personal statement is a delicious melting pot of Mexican American and authentic Mexican, seasoned with Italian overtones. Her public relations people are right: "Texans never tasted anything like this." Perhaps no other restaurant was as influential as Ninfa's in creating change. While some dishes may not be entirely new, she gave them a style and a presentation that put them on the map.

Ninfa's life story of hard work and determination to support her five children has become a Texas legend. She and her Italian husband, Tommy Laurenzo, began by manufacturing pizza dough, tortillas, chorizo, and Mexican cookies. It was this factory that housed the original ten-table Ninfa's, with Ninfa herself in the kitchen, creating the special sauces and recipes that would make her famous.

Although Ninfa began primarily with Mexican dishes, drawing on her knowledge of authentic recipes, her bold creativity soon branched out to include a few Italian touches. Not bound by tradition, Ninfa incorporated the best from every Mexican American dish she tasted—you'll find some California, a little New Mexico, and a lot of Texas pioneer spirit in her food. Her green sauce is her trademark, and her revival of the northern Mexican skirt steaks in flour tortillas—tacos al carbón—has become a classic.

As Ninfa has expanded to San Antonio, Dallas, and Arlington as well as Houston, she has been plagued by the problem all multimillion dollar chains ultimately face: consistency. But the fact remains, Ninfa is a Texas institution, an inspiration to many, living proof of an American dream come true. Her contributions to the food of Texas are a reality: she gave it a style and a flair felt far beyond the state.

THE TAVERN

Ruben and Carmela López
Crystal City

My search for the innovators of Mexican American food took me to many small Texas communities by car, by air, and sometimes by surprise! But I usually managed to dig up just another version of standard Tex-Mex . . . the rare spark of creativity was elusive.

One exception surfaced in South Texas, in a quaint little cafe that attracts people from miles around. The Tavern opened in 1945 and was discovered by the prestigious *Gourmet Restaurant Guide* of the fifties. Ruben and Carmela López bought the restaurant from its first owner, and they take great pride in preserving its original integrity—there were once many of these little cafes scattered throughout Texas, but few have remained, much less remained the same over the years.

What makes this unassuming cafe so special? For starters, it presents the most unusual chile con queso I've ever encountered. The sauces are homemade, rich, and full-bodied, but without the characteristic Tex-Mex taste that seems to flow from restaurant to restaurant. Each presentation has a reason . . . sometimes a matter of economics, sometimes based on sound cooking techniques, a quality often missing in other restaurants. Ruben and Carmela use many of the Tavern's original recipes but constantly improve on them, securing the freshest ingredients possible. The fruit cobblers are a good example. Carmela varies the cobblers, using the best seasonal fruits. She prepares the fruits first, with a technique which insures that they are not overcooked, then bakes the pastry separately. The result is fresh-tasting fruit and a crisp and flaky crust— a technique handed down for generations in her Mexican American family.

I hope that the Tavern's recipes will be preserved in this book. While their fame and fortune cannot equal that of recipes from the more flamboyant or highly visible chefs, they are the foundation upon which many of the popularized dishes rest.

TILA'S
Clive Duval
Houston

Clive Duval's résumé sounds like an entry in Ripley's "Believe It or Not." How does a boy from Rhode Island wind up creating Mexican food with a French twist?

Clive was educated in both the East and the West. He traveled extensively in Central America, where he spent four years growing sorghum, corn, black beans, and lemongrass, adding cities in Nicaragua, Honduras, and Guatemala to his list of hometowns. He ended his wanderings by entering restaurant management school in Philadelphia—thus being introduced to the world of fine French cooking. A devoted and creative cook, Clive wanted to show Houston an alternative to the standard Tex-Mex dishes.

Clive was brought up on swordfish—which is now one of his most popular mesquite-grilled dishes—in his native Rhode Island. He imports mesquite from Mexico; it's burned slowly for about a week, then chopped up into charcoal. Californians may think they discovered mesquite grilling, but Texans have been grilling their meals over mesquite for centuries. Clive's marinades and grilling techniques are unequaled in Houston. His research shows in Tila's succulent chicken, shrimp, or fajitas. Clive was one of the first to break away from the traditional Mexican restaurant decor—Tila's newly renovated art deco structure in the old Montrose area of Houston reflects his light, innovative style of food.

This dedicated chef may fly in lobster from Maine and serve it with Mexican Cream or cheeses. Or take a French sauce and give it Mexican seasoning. His tortillas, both whole wheat and the more traditional corn and flour, are delivered fresh daily. Fresh ingredients are emphasized in all dishes—even in marinades and beverages.

Clive experiments daily with specials, adding his creative flair to the fine cuisine at Tila's. His expert cooking techniques, dedication to his craft, innovative decor, and interesting combinations set this young chef apart from the crowd. Like Jesse and Carmen Calvillo at La Fogata, he has created a new atmosphere for Mexican American food as well as a new look and a more refined taste. Clive is a newcomer, but one to watch. His influence has just begun.

LA ESQUINA, LAS CANARIAS,
THE MANSION ON TURTLE CREEK

*I*nnovations and trends are often stimulated by privately owned, important hotels. Their restaurants and their adventurous clienteles pave the way for others. Three such hotels stand out in Texas.

La Esquina at the Dallas Loews Anatole, tucked into the corner of a spectacular atrium setting, serves an outstanding combination of regional Tex-Mex, inspired dishes from Mexico, and creative interpretations by its chef. Mariachis sing a traditional greeting from the sunny atrium lobby, luring conventioneers to sample some of the Mexican American specialties displayed on the colorful tables. Early in 1984, when the hotel doubled its size, another commitment to local cuisine was made in the Nana Grill. Mesquite-grilled specialties are accompanied by contemporary versions of regional dishes, featuring native ingredients in innovative presentations.

Las Canarias, at La Mansión del Río in a romantic San Antonio Riverwalk setting, honors the Canary Islanders who settled along these banks. The cuisine concept is Spanish, punctuated by flamenco dancers who perform nightly during the dinner hour. Regional Tex-Mex specialties are incorporated into both the Café del Sol and Las Canarias. Decor, atmosphere, and food blend into a single impression that emphasizes the culinary mix of Spanish and Mexican in San Antonio's history.

The Mansion on Turtle Creek, housed in Dallas' elegant Sheppard King Mansion, has been restored to its traditional European atmosphere and decorated with the kind of art that an international collector might bring to Texas. The food has been international, ranging from French in the beginning to a sophisticated blend of American and European. The Mansion is unique because it maintains a traditional European elegance while keeping a commitment to native ingredients and dishes. What began with Tortilla Soup and huevos rancheros has become an interesting mix of creative Southwestern cuisine, presented as elegantly as the surroundings.

Handling and Preparing Hot Chile Peppers

LA FOGATA
Center: La Fogata's Chile Strips
Far Right: Grilled Peppers With

Chicken
Bottom: Soft Chicken Tacos
Far Left: Tacos al Carbón

HANDLING AND PREPARING HOT CHILE PEPPERS

BE SURE TO READ THE COMPLETE INSTRUCTIONS BEFORE ROASTING THE CHILES.

CAUTION

When handling hot chile peppers, wear rubber gloves or generously oil your hands. Contact with the pepper oils will irritate the skin. Avoid rubbing your eyes because the oils will cause them to burn painfully.

Fresh Small Chiles (Jalapeño or Serrano)

Handle one at a time. With a sharp knife, cut away the stem; split the chile open. Remove the seeds with the tip of the knife. Pare away any large, fleshy veins. To make them somewhat less hot, soak prepared chiles in cold water for 1 hour. Or soak in a solution of 1 part each vinegar and water, a few tablespoons oil, and 1 teaspoon each sugar and salt. Refrigerate for a few days.

Canned Chiles

Rinse off the brine and seeds with cold water and pull away the stems before using the chiles.

To Roast Fresh Chiles and Sweet Red Peppers

Make a small slit in each chile and roast by one of the following methods.

1. *Gas Stove*

Spear the chiles with a long-handled fork and hold over the medium flame of a gas stove. Turn to be sure all the skin is charred. As long as the chiles are not left over the flame after blistered and charred, they will not burn. After they are completely blistered, rinse the skins off under cool water; then remove stems and seeds. The flesh will be bright green.

2.	*Electric Burner or Hot Plate*	Put 3 or 4 chiles at a time on a wire rack. Spear as in gas stove method. Place over a burner set on medium to medium-high. Use tongs to turn the chiles so all sides are blistered and charred. Place chiles in heat-proof plastic freezer storage bags and freeze for 10 minutes or until ready to use (2 weeks to 6 months). If using immediately, rinse and then cut away stems, split open, and remove seeds.
3.	*Broiler*	Preheat the broiler and set the chiles on a cookie sheet. Roast 4 to 6 inches away from heat source, turning to blister all sides. Transfer to plastic bags and freeze for 10 minutes or freeze as in preceding method.
4.	*Outdoor Grill*	Roast the chiles when the smoke has subsided and all scent of any charcoal starter has evaporated. Use the hottest portion of the fire, moving the grate as close to the coals as possible. Turn the chiles to be sure all exposed surfaces are blistered and well charred. Remove and place immediately in heatproof plastic bags and then freeze for 10 minutes. (This stops the cooking process and makes the skin peel easily.) When peppers are roasted in this way, they have a wonderful flavor.
5.	*Blowtorch*	Although it sounds a bit odd, this is my preferred method. Use a small propane torch, sometimes called a cook's torch. I am particularly fond of this method because the chiles stay firm and bright green. The torch easily reaches all the nooks and crannies, making the chiles easier to peel and more of the flesh usable. It is a superior method for chiles rellenos or the grilled chiles from La

Fogata. Spear the stem portion with a long-handled fork. Open the fuel valve about ⅛ of a turn, allowing just enough propane to escape. Use a cigarette lighter and, when lit, increase the propane to make a 1½-to-2-inch flame. Torch all exposed areas of the chile until well charred. Let cool, then rinse under cold water to remove all the peel. (If freezing, leave skin intact.) This method also works well with both tomatoes and red bell peppers, leaving a firm product that will be less mushy. All peppers will sauté beautifully with this technique.

TO PREPARE CHILES RELLENOS

Carefully make a slit down each chile and then, using scissors, cut away seeds and veins, taking care to leave the stem intact. Store in plastic bags until ready to use, no more than 12 hours.

FREEZING

Always freeze chiles with charred skins intact, double-wrapped in freezerproof plastic bags.

CHILES

NEW MEXICO GREEN CHILE

Many varieties with different names and degrees of hotness. Generally smaller than the California green chile, with a pointed tip, about 6–8 inches long, with a bright green color. Usually hot to hotter. Canned green chiles may be substituted (not jalapeños, which are smaller with a different flavor). These canned chiles are almost always milder; therefore, you may wish to add 1–2 jalapeño chiles to increase the hotness.

POBLANO CHILE

Large dark green chile, about the size of a green bell pepper, only narrower. Ranges from mild to hot, depending on the source and the season. No canned substitute.

CALIFORNIA ANAHEIM

Large green chile, about 8 inches long, with a rounded tip and thick flesh. Generally mild, though, when grown in the El Paso area, can be hotter. Bright green. Canned green chiles may be substituted.

YELLOW WAX CHILE

Small hot chile, about the size of a jalapeño. Use with restraint.

JALAPEÑO CHILE

Small hot chile, ranging from 2–4 inches. Large ones generally less hot. Not usually roasted and peeled; rather, used fresh in relishes, sauces, or garnishes. Canned jalapeños widely available and, though the color is less attractive, may be substituted.

SERRANO CHILE

Smaller than jalapeños, quite hot, though with a somewhat less harsh bite. Not usually roasted and peeled. Used for garnishes or salsas. Canned substitutes available.

CHILE ANCHO	The dried poblano with a wrinkled skin. This is the chile from which chile con carne is made. Moderately mild to medium-hot. The chile powder made from this chile is a deep brick red. Gebhardt's Chile Powder is made from the chile ancho.
CALIFORNIA CHILE (ALSO CALLED PASILLA)	Smooth skin, brick red in color. The powder made from this chile is a brighter red than that from the chile ancho. Used for sauces, particularly with enchiladas. Some canned sauces are available.
NEW MEXICO CHILE (ALSO CALLED RISTRA)	Usually a brighter red than the California chile and, if sun-dried, more translucent than other dried chiles. The powder made from these chiles is a bright red and always very hot. Some canned sauces are available made from this and the California chile, such as Las Palmas Red Chili Sauce.
CHILE CHIPOTLE	Dried chile (probably the jalapeño), canned in an orange-red, very hot sauce.
CHILE TEPÍN AND CHILE PEQUÍN	Small seedlike chiles originally used to preserve meats or to make beef jerky. Sometimes crushed and used in chile con carne or salsas.
PASILLA	Deep black, wrinkled-skin chile. Used in classic mole sauces along with chile ancho and other chiles. Not readily available.
JAPONE OR SERRANO SECO (ALSO CALLED CHILE DE ÁRBOL)	Small, dried, very hot chile with a smooth skin. Used to flavor sauces, added whole rather than blended into a sauce like the larger dried chiles. Common also in Chinese cooking.

CASCABEL CHILE

Smooth skin, red-brown in color. This small chile is used in both raw and cooked salsas. Cascabels are often difficult to obtain; California or ancho chiles can be substituted.

Relishes, Salsas, and Fillings

RELISHES, SALSAS, AND FILLINGS

Tila's Red Sauce	Tila's
Ninfa's Red Salsa	Ninfa's
Green Chile Salsa	La Hacienda
Pico de Gallo	Mariano's
Ernesto's Hot Sauce	Ernesto's
Chile and Cilantro Pesto	Author's Contribution
Green Chile Cream Sauce	Los Tres Bobos
Green Mole Sauce	Los Panchos
Mexican Cream	Author's Contribution
Tila's Cream Sauce	Tila's
Chicken Stew	Author's Contribution
Tila's Cream Sauce	Tila's

TILA'S RED SAUCE

Each restaurant has its own personal red sauce. Clive Duval uses this salsa both as an appetizer with tostados and as a sauce for many of his dishes. See the recipe for Tila's Poblano and Cheese Enchiladas (p. 148), prepared with this sauce.

5   medium-size tomatoes, cores intact
3   serrano chiles or 2 jalapeño chiles, stemmed and seeded
1   small white onion, finely chopped, or ½ bunch green onions, chopped
½   cup cilantro leaves, minced
3   tablespoons fresh lime juice
    salt and pepper to taste

On a lightly oiled cookie sheet about 4 inches from the broiling element, with the door ajar, broil the tomatoes, turning them until all surfaces are roasted. Do not worry if you have some charred or blackened areas. This takes about 20 minutes.

Add the chiles to the tomatoes during the last 5 to 8 minutes, grilling until blistered. Remove the peel from the tomatoes, and then transfer both tomatoes and chiles to a blender or a food processor fitted with a metal blade and process to roughly chop. You will have to do this in 4 batches. Take care not to liquefy or over-process.

Transfer the tomato mixture along with the remaining ingredients to a large skillet or saucepan and bring to a boil. Simmer, skimming the top as the foam rises, for about 20 to 25 minutes. Adjust the salt and pepper to taste.

STORAGE, FREEZING, AND ADVANCE PREPARATION

The sauce keeps for about 10 days, refrigerated, or it may be frozen 6 to 9 months.

NINFA'S RED SALSA

If good ripe, fresh tomatoes are not available, you may want to add some tomato sauce or the juice from canned Italian-style tomatoes when sautéing the salsa. Or substitute canned Italian-style tomatoes. It is not necessary to peel the tomatoes; however, this is a matter of personal preference.

1–2	*chiles de árboles* or *1–2 slender, hot, dried red peppers, such as japones*	Place the dried chiles on a cookie sheet and toast in a 325-degree oven for about 3 to 4 minutes. Stem and seed and set aside.
4	*medium-size tomatoes, halved*	In a medium-size skillet, simmer the tomatoes and garlic, in just enough water to prevent scorching, until softened—about 20 minutes. Transfer to a blender and puree along with the cilantro, salt, toasted chiles, and, if desired, jalapeños for 1 to 2 minutes.
3	*cloves garlic*	
4	*cilantro sprigs*	
1	*teaspoon salt*	
1–2	*jalapeño chiles (optional)*	
1–2	*tablespoons oil*	Sauté the pureed salsa in a skillet with hot oil for 1 to 2 minutes. If the salsa is pale, you may wish to add some tomato sauce to deepen the color.
½	*cup tomato sauce (optional)*	
STORAGE, FREEZING, AND ADVANCE PREPARATION		The salsa may be made in advance and either refrigerated or frozen.

GREEN CHILE SALSA

This New Mexico specialty may be served hot or cold, but either way it is fast becoming a Texas crowd pleaser. It is often served with chips, much as a Texas salsa, and in this way it disappears rapidly. It is best made in this quantity.

1	medium-size onion, chopped
1	tablespoon butter

In a large skillet, sauté the onion in butter until soft and translucent.

½	pound ground beef or pork
1	clove garlic, minced
1½	teaspoons salt or to taste
½	teaspoon ground cumin

Add the ground meat, garlic, and seasonings and sauté until the beef is cooked.

2	pounds mild to hot California Anaheim or New Mexico green chiles, roasted and peeled, chopped, or canned mild green chiles, rinsed, or New Mexico frozen green chiles
1	green tomato, minced
3	tomatilloes, finely chopped
1–2	tablespoons granulated sugar, depending on the type of chiles used
½	cup, more or less, chicken stock

Add the chiles, tomato, tomatilloes, sugar, and stock and simmer 15 to 20 minutes. Add more stock as necessary to prevent the meat or chiles from sticking. Taste and adjust seasonings. Canned chiles may require more salt or sugar.

Serve hot or cold.

VARIATION

If you add extra stock and cook 10 to 15 minutes more, this may be used as a sauce for enchiladas or chimichangas or as a stew. This will require more salt or sugar.

AUTHOR'S NOTE

A pound of chiles is equal to about 10 whole chiles. If you are using the 3-ounce cans of chiles, it takes about 8 cans to make 2 pounds, as called for above. Do not substitute jalapeños.

STORAGE, FREEZING, AND ADVANCE PREPARATION

The sauce may be made 2 to 3 days in advance; it freezes quite well.

PICO DE GALLO

This chopped relish has become so popular for a variety of dishes that to choose the best is nearly impossible. Recipes are all very much the same—some use jalapeños, some serranos. The key is to select the best possible tomatoes and the freshest cilantro.

2 green onions, chopped 1–2 tablespoons cilantro, chopped 1–3 jalapeño chiles, stemmed, seed- ed, and chopped	Combine the onions, cilantro, and jalapeños in a glass bowl.
2 cups (2–3 medium-size) toma- toes, peeled and diced ½ teaspoon salt or to taste 1 tablespoon vegetable oil	Add the tomatoes and mix together thoroughly. Adjust salt to taste, adding the oil to smooth out the sauce.
	Serve as a relish or salsa for other dishes or as a dip with tostados.
STORAGE, FREEZING, AND ADVANCE PREPARATION	This sauce does not keep well; it is best when made 2 to 3 hours before serving.

ERNESTO'S HOT SAUCE

This recipe is Ernesto's specialty and one of his most successful trade secrets. It is delicious served with tostados, chilled shrimp, grilled beef, or seafood appetizers.

15–16   (about 1 pound) tomatilloes, halved
1–2   teaspoons sugar
5   serrano chiles, stemmed and seeded
1   clove garlic, finely minced
2   tablespoons white vinegar

¾   cup cooking oil, heated
½   teaspoon salt or to taste

In a medium-size saucepan, bring the tomatilloes, sugar, serranos, garlic, and vinegar to a boil. Simmer 8 to 10 minutes.

Transfer the cooked tomatillo mixture to a blender. Process until smooth and light in consistency—about 2 minutes. Then, while the machine is still running, pour the oil through the feed tube. When all the oil has been added, adjust salt to taste.

Serve the sauce either hot or cold.

STORAGE, FREEZING, AND ADVANCE PREPARATION

The sauce loses its texture with freezing but keeps well for 2 weeks refrigerated. Reblend, if necessary, to restore texture.

CHILE AND CILANTRO PESTO

This unusual pesto is a delicious change from refried beans on nachos, or it may be spread atop grilled chicken or fish. Mix it with equal amounts of sour cream as a dip for chips or seafood.

2   *poblano chiles, roasted and peeled*
1   *cup cilantro sprigs, loosely packed*

1–2 *cloves garlic, minced*
3   *ounces Parmesan cheese, finely grated*
⅓   *cup almonds or pine nuts, finely ground*
2–3 *tablespoons vegetable oil*
¼   *teaspoon salt (optional)*

VARIATION

STORAGE, FREEZING, AND ADVANCE PREPARATION

Using a blender or food processor, turn the machine on and off to finely chop the chiles and cilantro.

Add the garlic, cheese, and ground nuts; then add enough oil to make an easily spread mixture. Add salt if desired.

Store refrigerated or frozen until ready to use.

You may use mild green chiles in place of poblano chiles, or omit the chiles and make a cilantro pesto.

This sauce will keep well for 1½ weeks in the refrigerator, and it may be frozen.

GREEN CHILE CREAM SAUCE

Use this sauce with chicken enchiladas, grilled chicken or shrimp, or omelets or as a dip for fried vegetables.

2	*3-ounce cans green chiles* or *5 California Anaheim green chiles, roasted and peeled*
1/4	*cup onion, finely chopped*
1	*tablespoon butter*

Finely chop the green chiles. Then, using a medium-size skillet, sauté the onion and chiles in butter until the onions are soft and translucent—about 8 to 10 minutes. Set aside.

1	*cup milk*
1/2	*cup whipping cream*
1	*cup water*

Bring the milk, cream, and water to a boil.

1/4	*cup less 1 tablespoon flour*
1/4	*stick melted butter* or *margarine*
1/2	*tablespoon cilantro, finely chopped*

Transfer the chile mixture, flour, remaining butter, and cilantro to a blender or a food processor fitted with a metal blade. With the machine running, pour 1 cup of the hot milk mixture through the center and process until smooth.

Return the puree to the same saucepan with the remaining milk mixture and stir to thicken and cook the flour, about 5 minutes.

1/2	*teaspoon salt*
1/8	*teaspoon white pepper*
1/2	*jigger white wine*

Stir in salt, pepper, and white wine and cover, allowing the wine to blend with the sauce for 1 to 2 minutes. Remove from heat.

VARIATION

You can turn this into a delicious soup by adding 1 cup chicken stock and 1 cup corn kernels mashed with 1/2 cup heavy cream. Garnish with diced red pepper.

STORAGE, FREEZING, AND ADVANCE PREPARATION

The sauce may be made ahead and refrigerated 1 or 2 days.

GREEN MOLE SAUCE

At the restaurant, the sauce is prepared using a blender, which makes a very smooth sauce. You may prefer to substitute mild green chiles for fresh poblanos. You should feel free to use any combination of greens, letting personal taste be your guide.

2 small *poblano chiles, roasted and peeled* 1 *serrano chile, stemmed and seeded* 1 *cup lettuce, chopped* ½ *cup radish greens* or *spinach greens* ½ *cup fresh parsley* ½ *cup cilantro, loosely packed* 2 *epazote sprigs*	In a blender or a food processor fitted with a metal blade, process the chiles with the lettuce, greens, and herbs.
1 *onion, finely chopped* 1 *clove garlic, minced* 1–2 *tablespoons vegetable oil*	In a medium-size skillet, sauté the onion and garlic in vegetable oil for 5 to 8 minutes. Add the chile mixture and cook 10 to 15 minutes over medium-low heat. Set aside.
1–2 *tablespoons vegetable oil* 1 *small roll* or *slice stale bread, cubed* 3–4 *crisp nacho chips* ¼ *cup pumpkin seeds* 1½ *cups chicken stock* *salt to taste*	In a small skillet, heat the vegetable oil and sauté the bread cubes, nacho chips, and pumpkin seeds until golden brown. Transfer to a food processor fitted with a metal blade. Process to finely chop and then run the machine, adding the chicken stock. Add to the chile mixture and simmer 15 to 20 minutes, adding more stock if necessary. Adjust salt to taste.
VARIATION	For a lighter sauce with a more subtle flavor, whisk in ½ cup cream just prior to serving or when reheating.
STORAGE, FREEZING, AND ADVANCE PREPARATION	Store refrigerated or freeze until ready to use. This is best made 3 to 4 hours before serving.

MEXICAN CREAM

This is similar to a French *crème fraîche* and may be used as a substitute for sour cream. It will not curdle as easily as sour cream and is therefore excellent for topping enchiladas.

2 cups sour cream 1 cup heavy cream 2 teaspoons fresh lime juice	Stir ingredients together and let stand at room temperature for 2 hours. Refrigerate till ready to use. This will keep for 2 weeks.

CHICKEN STEW

This savory filling, similar to Ninfa's, may be used in tacos, flautas, enchiladas, or toasted and buttered bolillos. My favorite way is to prepare a light, warm chicken salad, using fresh lettuce and garnishes of white Mexican cheese (the crumbly variety like farmer cheese) and fresh slices of papaya, avocado, or tomato. This makes a large quantity; half the recipe fills 12 enchiladas. It freezes quite well; however, you may wish to halve the recipe.

2	*whole chickens*
1	*bay leaf*
2	*teaspoons salt*
2	*cloves garlic*
1	*onion slice*
	several cilantro sprigs

In a large (4-quart) stockpot, cover the chicken with water and then add the bay leaf, salt, garlic, onion, and cilantro. Bring to a boil and then simmer until the chicken is tender, about 50 minutes. Remove the chicken and strain and reserve the stock. The stock may be used for a soup base or sauce; it freezes well.

When it is cool enough to handle, debone and shred the chicken.

1	*medium-size onion, chopped*
2–3	*tablespoons vegetable oil*
3	*tomatoes, peeled and chopped, including juice*
1	*4-ounce can green chiles, chopped*
¼	*teaspoon salt*
¼	*teaspoon black pepper*
1–2	*teaspoons chile powder*
½	*teaspoon garlic powder*
¼–½	*cup chicken stock, if needed*

In a large (12-inch) skillet or sauté pan, sauté the onion in oil until soft and translucent, about 5 minutes. Stir in the chopped tomatoes, chiles, and seasonings; then add the chicken. Return to a boil (if using chilled chicken); then cook over medium heat for 3 to 5 minutes. You may need to add a small amount of chicken stock to keep the mixture moist.

AUTHOR'S NOTE

Shred chicken while still warm and shred with the grain. After chicken is refrigerated, it becomes too gelatinous to shred well. Storing chicken in some of its stock will keep it tender and moist.

STORAGE, FREEZING, AND ADVANCE PREPARATION

This filling may be refrigerated or frozen.

TILA'S CREAM SAUCE

This is Clive Duval's version of Mexican Cream. As it uses milk in place of cream, it is slightly less rich. Many restaurants use a similar substitution. Serve this sauce in place of sour cream for topping enchiladas or garnishing your favorite tortilla specialties.

1   cup sour cream
1   cup milk, preferably whole
2   tablespoons fresh lime juice
     salt and pepper to taste

Stir together all ingredients, adjusting salt and pepper to taste. Let stand at room temperature for 2 hours; then refrigerate until ready to use.

STORAGE, FREEZING, AND ADVANCE PREPARATION

This may be made several days in advance; it keeps refrigerated for about 7 to 10 days.

FROM MARIANO MARTÍNEZ

If salsa is at the end of its fresh peak, bring it to a boil and simmer for 15 minutes. Cool, adjust seasonings, and it will keep for several more days.

FROM ERNESTO TORRES

Add 1 teaspoon of vinegar to your fresh salsas. This helps increase their refrigeration life.

Brunch Dishes

LA HACIENDA
New Mexican Enchiladas/Avocado
Garnish (egg on top)/Salsa on the Side
Center of table: 3 salsas:
Green Chile Salsa
Salsa Cruda (no recipe)

Salsa Ranchero (no recipe)
Far left & right:
Chimichangas/Tomato Garnish
Center of table:
Sopaipillas/Honey

BRUNCH DISHES

YUCATÁN QUICHE

THE CRUST

¾–1 cup safflower oil
7–8 corn tortillas

In a medium-size skillet, heat the safflower oil. Dip each tortilla briefly to soften and seal and then press between paper towels.

Spray a 9-inch pie pan with a nonstick vegetable coating and then line with the prepared tortillas, overlapping them, extending about ½ inch over the pan edge.

THE FILLING

2   eggs
2   cups half-and-half or cream
½   teaspoon salt

2   cups (about 8 ounces) shredded Monterey jack cheese
1   cup refried beans
½   pound sausage, cooked and drained
2   tablespoons mild green chiles, diced

In a small bowl, combine the eggs, half-and-half or cream, and salt. Set aside.

Sprinkle half the cheese over the tortillas, followed by the beans, sausage, chiles, and then the egg mixture. Evenly distribute the remaining cheese over the top. Bake in a preheated 350-degree oven for 30 minutes or until firm.

PRESENTATION

1   avocado, diced
1   tomato, sliced
      snipped cilantro leaves

Garnish the baked quiche with avocado and tomato slices. Place cilantro leaves over the top. Serve warm.

STORAGE, FREEZING, AND ADVANCE PREPARATION

This is as good at room temperature as it is hot, but it does not freeze very well.

EGGS MAXIMILIAN

Cappy's flavorful sauce is prepared without butter or oil, which makes it a low-calorie sauce, perfect for eggs, chicken, fish, or grilled meats. To save preparation time, you may use crisp tortilla shells or toasted English muffins in place of masa cups. If fresh masa is not easy to obtain, use masa harina, adding 1 teaspoon sugar and 1 tablespoon cornmeal to the package directions.

THE RANCHERO SAUCE

1	2½-pound can whole tomatoes
1	onion, chopped
1	bell pepper, seeded and chopped
4	cloves garlic, minced
3	tomatoes, chopped
3–4	serrano chiles, finely minced
	snipped cilantro
1	cup water
4	ounces tomato paste
1½	teaspoons salt or to taste
½	teaspoon black pepper
½	teaspoon leaf oregano
½	teaspoon ground cumin

Drain all the juice from the canned tomatoes into a large saucepan. Roughly chop the tomatoes, combine with all the other vegetables, and bring to a boil.

Add water, tomato paste, and seasonings and return to a boil. Reduce heat and simmer for 20 minutes.

THE POACHED EGGS

1	poached egg per serving
	butter

Poach the eggs and hold them at room temperature, brushed with butter, while preparing the masa cups.

THE FRESH MASA

fresh corn masa (about 1 ounce per mold)
peanut oil for frying

Spray 3-inch fluted tin molds with a nonstick vegetable coating. Pinch off a ball of masa and then press into molds. Deep-fry, using tongs, in oil heated to 375 degrees. The molds will sink to the bottom and, as the masa cooks, it will separate from the molds and float. Turn to fry both sides. Take care not to overcook or the masa cups may become tough. Drain on paper towels.

ASSEMBLY AND PRESENTATION

grated Cheddar cheese
chopped fresh parsley

Use one poached egg per masa cup. Ladle sauce over each egg. Top with Cheddar cheese and place 4 inches under the broiling element, just long enough to melt the cheese.

Garnish with chopped parsley. Serve with fresh sliced fruit and seasonal berries.

STORAGE, FREEZING, AND ADVANCE PREPARATION

The sauce may be made a day ahead or several weeks ahead and frozen. The eggs may be poached the night before (if preparing for a large crowd), removed from the poaching liquid when slightly undercooked, and then held in ice-cold water overnight. Reheat by submerging in hot water about 1 minute and 20 seconds. The masa shells are best when made just prior to serving.

TEX-MEX CAPIROTADA

This is a most unusual combination as well as technique for this Tex-Mex bread pudding. When I first assembled it, it smelled like banana cream pie . . . a bit rich for dessert, unless served in very small portions. It makes an excellent brunch buffet item, served with whipped cream.

THE PUDDING MIXTURE

12	slices stale bread, preferably French or whole wheat
8–10	ounces grated Monterey jack or cubed cream cheese
¾	cup pitted prunes, plumped in hot water and diced
¾	cup seedless white raisins or dates, diced
2	large bananas, sliced, or coarsely chopped apples
1	cup sliced almonds

Toast the bread and allow to cool. Using a well-buttered baking dish, 12 by 9 by 2 inches, make a layer of bread, using about half the bread. Top with half the cheese and fruits and all the bananas or apples. Add another bread layer, then the remaining cheese, fruits, and the nuts. Set aside.

THE SYRUP

2	cups water
1½	cups brown sugar, packed
½	teaspoon cinnamon

In a medium-size saucepan, boil the water, sugar, and cinnamon together for 5 minutes. Pour over the pudding mixture.

THE EGG MIXTURE AND TOPPING

2	cups water
1	cup granulated sugar
4	eggs, separated
4	tablespoons flour

In the same saucepan, boil the water and sugar for 5 minutes. Remove 1 cup and beat with egg yolks and flour, then add this egg mixture to the remaining syrup and cook over medium heat, stirring constantly, for 5 minutes or until thick. Pour this custard over the bread and fruits.

Cover and let stand several hours at room temperature, or refrigerate overnight.

MARIANO'S

THE MERINGUE

	reserved egg whites
2	*tablespoons granulated sugar*

When ready to bake the pudding, beat the egg whites until very stiff, beating in the sugar at the last. Spread atop the pudding and then bake at 350 degrees for about 40 minutes, or until the meringue is well browned and the pudding is set.

PRESENTATION

sweetened whipped cream or *ice cream*

Serve small portions with a dollop of ice cream or whipped cream.

STORAGE, FREEZING, AND ADVANCE PREPARATION

The basic dessert, excluding the topping, may be prepared 24 hours in advance or overnight. Because of the sweet syrups, the bananas will not turn brown any faster than they would during ordinary baking. The topping should be added just prior to baking. The pudding may be served either hot or cold; it will reheat easily without changing consistency, either in a microwave oven or in a hot 400-degree oven, covered with foil.

NEW MEXICAN ENCHILADAS

This dish is one of my favorites for brunch, lunch, or dinner. The enchiladas are stacked like pancakes and topped with an egg. Because the New Mexico sundried red chile pod is difficult to obtain, I have given a method which uses a canned enchilada sauce. Though not traditional, fresh tomatoes tame the sauce, which may be prepared in advance.

1   small onion, chopped
1½   cups Monterey jack cheese, grated
1½   cups Cheddar cheese, grated

Using a strainer, rinse the onion with cold water to remove all bitterness. Toss the cheese and onion together. Set aside.

½   small onion, chopped (optional)
1–2   tablespoons vegetable oil
1   1-pound can tomatoes, crushed
2   tomatoes, peeled and chopped
1–1½ cups chicken stock
1½   teaspoons salt
½   teaspoon garlic powder
½   teaspoon ground cumin
1   teaspoon leaf oregano
1–1½ cups canned enchilada sauce
4–5   tablespoons tomato paste, if needed

       vegetable oil
1   dozen corn tortillas

Sauté the onion, if using, in 1–2 tablespoons hot oil for 10 to 12 minutes. Add the drained canned tomatoes and the fresh tomatoes and transfer to a blender or a food processor to puree. Return the puree to a medium-size saucepan and stir in the chicken stock, seasonings, and the enchilada sauce. Cook 30 minutes, stirring occasionally. As the sauce simmers and reduces, it will thicken. If necessary, stir in tomato paste to thicken further.

In a medium-size skillet, heat oil to about 300 degrees. Pass tortillas into hot oil for a few seconds to soften and seal. Remove carefully and set aside between paper towels. Do this just prior to assembly.

ASSEMBLY AND
PRESENTATION

Put a layer of the combined cheese and onion on a softened tortilla. Top with another tortilla and another layer of cheese and onion, ending with a third tortilla.

Pour the sauce on the layered tortillas. Heat in a 350-degree oven until warm, with the cheese slightly melted.

4 *eggs*
   taco sauce (optional)

Meanwhile, either poach or fry the eggs. To serve, top each tortilla stack with an egg. Top with a small spoonful of the cheese mixture and serve with taco sauce, if desired.

AUTHOR'S NOTE

The New Mexico red chile paste that La Hacienda uses is not readily available. You may substitute canned enchilada sauce, adding 1 tablespoon pure-ground, red New Mexico chile powder. Sauté the powder first in 1−2 tablespoons vegetable oil over medium-low heat for 1 to 2 minutes to remove the bitter taste. Chile ancho pods or Gebhardt's chile powder do not have the same taste. The canned red chile or enchilada sauce is usually made with the New Mexico chile, and, while you may not like these sauces alone, they do make a good base when mixed with fresh ingredients and seasonings.

STORAGE, FREEZING, AND ADVANCE PREPARATION

The sauce may be prepared several days in advance; it freezes well.

CHILE QUICHE

This dish could be simplified by using corn tortillas for the crust, as in Bennie Ferrell's Yucatán Quiche (see p. 51). When I first tested this recipe, I thought it too simple and ordinary to include in this book . . . that is, until my son and his food critic friends devoured it. I immediately understood why it is a caterer's favorite!

1	*deep-dish pastry shell*	Preheat the oven to 400 degrees. Without puncturing the crust, bake the shell for 10 minutes; then remove and cool. Reduce the temperature to 375 degrees. If using a frozen pastry shell, you will need to reduce the half-and-half in the filling, as the prepared shells are smaller. Reduce the cooking time as well by 15 minutes.
2	*avocados, mashed*	In a small bowl, combine the avocados with garlic, lemon juice, tomato, half the chiles, and pepper sauce. Refrigerate until ready to use.
1	*clove garlic, minced*	
3	*tablespoons fresh lemon juice*	
1	*tomato, peeled, seeded, and chopped*	
4	*fresh green chiles, roasted and peeled, or 1 4-ounce can mild green chiles (not jalapeños), seeded and chopped*	
1/4	*teaspoon hot pepper sauce*	
1/2	*pound ground beef*	In a medium-size skillet, sauté the beef, onion, remaining chiles, and seasoning for about 12 to 15 minutes or until the onion is soft and translucent. Drain and discard all excess fat.
1/4	*cup onion, chopped*	
1–2	*tablespoons taco-seasoning mix or chile powder*	
3	*eggs, slightly beaten*	In a small bowl, combine the eggs, half-and-half, and seasonings.
1 1/2	*cups half-and-half*	
1/2	*teaspoon salt*	
1/8	*teaspoon pepper*	
1 1/2	*cups (about 6 ounces) shredded Cheddar cheese*	Place the grated cheese in the shell, topped by the drained beef and the egg mixture. Bake for 35 to 40 minutes at 375 degrees or until set.

BENNIE FERRELL

PRESENTATION

chopped tomatoes

Serve the quiche in wedges accompanied by the avocado relish and topped with chopped tomatoes.

shredded lettuce
nacho chips (optional)

Garnish with shredded lettuce and nacho chips, if desired.

STORAGE, FREEZING, AND ADVANCE PREPARATION

This quiche is also as good cold as it is hot, and it makes an excellent picnic item. Prepare it the same day you plan to serve it.

SPINACH AND GREEN CHILES IN TORTILLA CUPS

This is my favorite Southwestern vegetable, and it is surprisingly easy to prepare. Be sure to see the variation at the end for a most spectacular brunch dish.

THE FILLING

2   packages frozen spinach, thawed
3–4   mild green chiles, roasted and peeled
½   medium-size onion, chopped
1   tablespoon butter

3   ounces Parmesan or Monterey jack cheese, grated
½   cup sour cream
2   eggs
2   egg yolks
     pinch of coriander
     pinch of red pepper
½   teaspoon salt or to taste

Place the thawed spinach in a tea towel (preferably an old one), and then close and twist to wring all the moisture from the spinach. Do not skip this important step. Finely chop the green chiles and set aside. In a small skillet, sauté the onion in butter until soft and translucent.

Combine the spinach with the chiles, onion, two-thirds of the cheese, sour cream, eggs, egg yolks, and seasonings. Set aside while preparing the shells. (For a lighter, soufflé result, reserve the 2 egg whites, and whip very stiff, then fold into the spinach prior to baking.)

THE SHELLS

½   cup safflower oil
½   stick butter
10–12 very thin corn tortillas

Spray 2 muffin tins with a nonstick vegetable coating. Heat the oil and butter in an 8-inch skillet to about 300 degrees. Dip a tortilla for 20 to 30 seconds, then lift to allow excess oil to run off. Immediately press into muffin tins to make a container. Repeat with the remaining tortillas, alternating every other muffin cup.

ASSEMBLY

Spoon the filling into the shells and top with the remaining cheese. Bake at 375 degrees for 20 to 25 minutes or until set. If the edges become too brown, cover with foil.

VARIATION

You may turn this into a delightful brunch dish for 12. Use 12 tortillas in place of 10, dividing the filling between them. Top each filled tortilla with 1 raw egg (at room temperature). Add the cheese during the final 5 minutes of baking time, when the eggs are nearly set. Serve the eggs with your favorite tomato sauce, Tila's Red Sauce (see p. 37), or Ninfa's Red Salsa (see p. 38).

STORAGE, FREEZING, AND ADVANCE PREPARATION

You may prepare the filling early in the day; however, the shells are best prepared no more than 4 hours before baking. These freeze quite well. Reduce the baking time by 10 minutes, cool, and freeze double-wrapped in plastic. Thaw before reheating, and then reheat in a standard oven or microwave.

GAZPACHO OMELET

Unusual and surprisingly refreshing.

1	tablespoon butter or margarine
¼	cup cucumber, peeled and chopped
¼	cup tomatoes, chopped
2	tablespoons onion, chopped
2	tablespoons green bell pepper, chopped

In an 8-inch omelet pan or skillet, melt 1 tablespoon butter or margarine. Add the cucumber, tomatoes, onion, and green pepper. Cook over medium-high heat until the onion and pepper are tender, stirring occasionally. Keep warm while preparing omelets.

4	extralarge or 6 medium-size eggs
2	tablespoons water
½	teaspoon salt
⅛	teaspoon pepper
	dash of hot pepper sauce

In a small bowl, combine the eggs, water, salt, pepper, and hot pepper sauce. Beat with a fork or whisk until mixed well but not frothy.

2	tablespoons butter or margarine
½	cup shredded Monterey jack cheese

In the same size omelet pan or skillet, melt 1 tablespoon butter or margarine over medium-high heat. When a drop of water sizzles in the pan, pour in half the egg mixture. Cook, gently lifting edges so uncooked portion flows underneath, until eggs are soft but set. Spoon half the vegetable mixture onto omelet, covering only half the omelet. Fold one side over to cover the filling and then slide onto a serving plate. Top with half the cheese and keep warm while preparing the second omelet.

PRESENTATION

Tila's Red Sauce (see p. 37) or Ninfa's Red Salsa (see p. 38) chopped avocado

Garnish the omelets with fresh salsa and chopped avocado. Accompany with a medley of fresh fruits such as cantaloupe, honeydew melon, strawberries, and papaya.

STORAGE, FREEZING, AND ADVANCE PREPARATION

The omelets cannot be prepared in advance.

BENNIE FERRELL

FROM CAPPY LAWTON

Make an interesting breakfast or luncheon sandwich by using bolillos. You can split them, remove the doughy center portion, then generously butter and toast them under a broiler. They will be very crisp and may be stuffed with your favorite chicken, picadillo, or fajita filling.

You can create a wonderful finger food by removing the end, so you have a cone shape. Scoop out the dough, use a brush to butter the inside, and then warm in a hot oven. Add your favorite breakfast or lunch filling. Makes a terrific buffet item your guests will remember for a long time.

Appetizers and Snacks

ANNE GREER'S
Left—Top to Bottom: Sangría Mousse
(Bennie Ferrell Catering)
Capirotada (Author's Contribution)
Dessert Cobblers (The Tavern)
Yucatán Quiche (Bennie Ferrell

Catering)
Far Right—Top to Bottom: Corn Soup
(Cafe Cancún)
Scallops with Chile Cream Sauce
(Cappy's)
Portuguese Tortillas (The Tavern)

APPETIZERS AND SNACKS

Ernesto's Ceviche — Ernesto's
Oyster and Clam Ceviche — Las Canarias
Cappy's Ceviche — Cappy's
Portuguese Tortillas — The Tavern
Diablitos — La Esquina
Fried Avocados — Cappy's
Mexican Layered Dip — Bennie Ferrell Catering
La Fogata's Chile Strips — La Fogata
Crabmeat Nachos — Ernesto's
Highland Park Nachos — Mariano's
Chicken or Shrimp Nachos — Author's Contribution
Seafood Cheese — Ninfa's
Ham and Cheese — Ninfa's
Chihuahua Cheese — Ninfa's

ERNESTO'S CEVICHE

Be sure to use only fresh fish for ceviche. If you are uncertain whether the fish has been frozen, drop it into boiling water for a minute before marinating. I have included several versions of this popular appetizer, each one slightly different.

THE FISH

12	medium-size fresh shrimp, peeled and deveined
12	fresh sea scallops

Blanch both shrimp and scallops 1½ minutes in boiling water. Drain and cut in small pieces and place in a glass bowl.

THE SAUCE

½–¾	cup fresh lime or lemon juice
1	tomato, chopped
1	small yellow onion, chopped
1	jalapeño chile, stemmed, seeded, and diced
2	tablespoons cilantro, chopped
2	tablespoons tomato catsup
5–6	drops Tabasco sauce

Add enough fresh lime or lemon juice to cover, then add vegetables, cilantro, catsup, and Tabasco.

Refrigerate, covered, for at least 3 hours before serving.

PRESENTATION

8	lettuce leaves
1	avocado, sliced
8	nacho chips

Spoon the ceviche over lettuce leaves and garnish with an avocado slice. Serve with nacho chips.

STORAGE, FREEZING, AND ADVANCE PREPARATION

The recipe is best prepared a day in advance; it will keep 3 days under refrigeration.

OYSTER AND CLAM CEVICHE

THE FISH

12	*large fresh oysters*
16	*large fresh clams*
	juice of 3 large limes
	pinch of salt
1	*cup green onions, sliced*
½	*cup cilantro, chopped*
½	*jalapeño chile, minced*
	pinch of white pepper

In a glass bowl, combine all ingredients and marinate for at least 2 hours.

THE SAUCE

2	*cups V-8 juice*
1	*cup tomato catsup*
1	*tablespoon salad oil*
1	*teaspoon cider vinegar*

After 2 hours or not more than 4, add the V-8 juice, catsup, oil, and vinegar to the fish mixture. Marinate at least 1 more hour before serving.

PRESENTATION

romaine lettuce leaves
lime wedges
avocado chunks (optional)

Line champagne glasses with lettuce. Arrange the ceviche in the glasses, garnished with lime wedges and avocado chunks, if desired.

STORAGE, FREEZING, AND ADVANCE PREPARATION

This may be prepared up to 8 hours in advance, but it should be used within 12 hours.

CAPPY'S CEVICHE

Cappy uses redfish; however, you may substitute Gulf red snapper, halibut, or swordfish.

THE FISH

1	*pound fresh sea scallops*
1	*pound fresh redfish filets*
	juice of 8 lemons (about 2 cups)

Cut the scallops and redfish into even pieces, approximately half an inch square. Add to lemon juice, making sure that all the pieces are well coated. Refrigerate in a glass container for 3 to 4 hours or more, stirring occasionally. The lemon juice will "cook" the fish.

THE SAUCE

½	*yellow onion, finely chopped*
¼	*cup tomato paste*
½	*cup V-8 juice*
1–2	*teaspoons salt*
½	*cup green olives, chopped*
2	*tablespoons Worcestershire sauce*
1	*teaspoon Tabasco sauce*
3	*large tomatoes, seeded and chopped*
1	*tablespoon fresh parsley, minced*
1	*tablespoon cilantro, minced*
2	*serrano chiles, seeded and finely chopped*

Meanwhile, using another bowl, combine the sauce ingredients. Stir gently with a spatula until the mixture is uniform. Refrigerate until ready to use.

Using a slotted spoon, remove the fish from its marinade. Discard all but ¾ cup juice. Stir to mix all ingredients and refrigerate.

PRESENTATION

2	*heads Bibb lettuce*
	snipped cilantro
	sliced avocado
	lime wedges

Serve the ceviche on several lettuce leaves, and garnish each portion with cilantro, an avocado slice, and lime wedges.

STORAGE, FREEZING, AND ADVANCE PREPARATION

This ceviche may be prepared up to 8 hours in advance, but it should be used within 12 hours.

PORTUGUESE TORTILLAS

This unusual presentation, developed by Carmela López, takes a traditional chile con queso recipe and injects it with flair and pizzazz.

THE TORTILLA CHIPS

12 *corn tortillas*
    peanut oil for frying

Cut four round corners, about 1½ inches wide, from each tortilla. Once cut, halve these to make strips. Deep-fry the removed portion in hot peanut oil until crisp. Set aside. Reserve the center portion for chalupas.

THE SAUCE

1 *recipe enchilada sauce (see p. 142)*

Prepare the enchilada sauce and set aside.

THE VEGETABLES

2   *stalks celery, coarsely chopped*
1   *yellow onion, chopped*
1   *bell pepper, coarsely chopped*
     beef or *chicken stock (optional)*
1–2 *tablespoons butter (optional)*
2   *tomatoes, peeled and diced*
     salt and pepper to taste

In a medium-size skillet, simmer all the vegetables in enough beef or chicken stock to cover, or sauté in butter until tender. Stir in the tomatoes and season with salt and pepper to taste. Drain off excess fat or stock and then set vegetables aside.

ASSEMBLY AND PRESENTATION

Mound the crisp tortilla chips on a serving platter or plate about 10 to 12 inches in diameter.

2 *cups Cheddar or Monterey jack cheese, grated*

In a medium-size saucepan, reheat the enchilada sauce and then add the grated cheese by spoonfuls, stirring constantly until smooth. The sauce will be moderately thick.

Stir in the drained vegetables and then spoon the sauce over the tortillas.

   fresh minced parsley or *minced cilantro (optional)*

Garnish with minced parsley or cilantro, if desired.

STORAGE, FREEZING, AND
ADVANCE PREPARATION

Both the sauce and the tortillas may
be prepared in advance. If you have
a food processor, process the sauce
after adding the cheese for several
seconds, in two batches, to insure a
smooth, velvety mixture.

DIABLITOS

La Esquina makes these little devils with cod; however, for ease of preparation I have substituted tuna fish. If you prefer a milder dish, substitute canned green chiles, using a toothpick to enclose the filling.

THE SAUCE

2	tablespoons all-purpose flour
6	ounces Cheddar cheese, finely shredded
4	ounces Monterey jack cheese, finely shredded
3½	ounces cream cheese, at room temperature
1	cup half-and-half, heated to the boiling point

This sauce is easily made smooth, with consistent results, when a food processor is used. You may use a blender; however, you will need to do the job in 3 batches.

With the metal blade in place, process the flour and cheeses to a paste consistency. With the machine running, pour the hot liquid through the feed tube. Scrape down the sides of the bowl and then transfer mixture to a saucepan; stir constantly over medium heat for 2 to 3 minutes until smooth and thick.

¼	cup onion, chopped
1	tablespoon butter
1	tablespoon pimiento, chopped

In a small skillet, sauté the onion in butter until soft and translucent. Add pimiento and stir into the cheese sauce.

THE CHILES

3	dozen jalapeño chiles, stems intact

Rinse the jalapeños. (The jalapeños may be tempered somewhat by a preliminary 30-minute soaking in cold water. Rinse well before stuffing.) Using scissors, make a small slit halfway down each chile, just long enough to allow the filling to be inserted. Cut away the seeds.

THE FILLING

2	7-ounce cans water-packed tuna fish, drained
1	cup ricotta cheese
2	tablespoons Parmesan cheese, grated

In a small bowl, blend together the filling ingredients.

2	tablespoons cilantro, chopped
1	teaspoon leaf oregano
¼	teaspoon ground cumin
1–1½	teaspoons salt or to taste
1	tablespoon fresh lime juice
3	tablespoons sour cream

Stuff all the prepared jalapeños. Then either refrigerate until ready to fry or prepare the batter and fry immediately.

THE BATTER

2	eggs, separated
1–2	tablespoons flour
⅛	teaspoon salt

In a small bowl, beat the egg whites until stiff.

In another bowl, using the same beaters, beat the egg yolks, flour, and salt about a minute until pale yellow and thick. Then beat the yolks into the whites.

ASSEMBLY AND PRESENTATION

peanut oil for frying

Dip each prepared chile in the batter. Then, using tongs, deep-fry in oil at 375 degrees until crisp and golden, about 1 minute. Drain on a paper towel while preparing the rest of the chiles.

Serve in a chafing dish over hot water with the sauce available for dipping.

VARIATION

If using the mild green chiles, you may wish to add 1–2 minced jalapeño chiles to the onion and pimiento sauté.

STORAGE, FREEZING, AND ADVANCE PREPARATION

The chiles may be stuffed 8 hours ahead and then refrigerated until you are ready to fry them. When fried, they will keep for about 1 to 2 hours on a warm platter. The sauce may be made several days in advance and refrigerated. It will become quite thick and solid upon refrigeration but melts easily.

FRIED AVOCADOS

Serve these with a spicy tomato salsa or any salsa of your choice. I have tried them also as an accompaniment to grilled fish . . . unusual, very Texas, and always a conversation piece.

THE SEASONING SALT

¼ cup salt	Combine all ingredients and set aside.
1 tablespoon coarse-ground black pepper	
1–2 teaspoons garlic powder	
1½ teaspoons paprika	

THE SEASONED FLOUR

1½ cups all-purpose flour	Thoroughly mix together the flour with additional seasonings and set in a shallow plate. Set the remaining seasoning salt aside for the avocados.
⅛ cup seasoning salt	
½ tablespoon chile powder	
2 teaspoons ground cumin	

THE BATTER

1 cup buttermilk	In a small mixing bowl, combine the batter ingredients and mix until smooth. Set aside and let rest for at least 30 minutes, at room temperature.
1 egg, beaten	
½ cup water	
½ cup all-purpose flour	
2 tablespoons vegetable oil	

ASSEMBLY AND PRESENTATION

peanut oil for frying	Heat the peanut oil, at least 3 inches deep, to 375 degrees. 30 minutes before frying the avocados, cut and sprinkle them with lemon juice. Dust lightly with seasoning salt. Dip first in the wet batter, then dredge in the seasoned flour. Dip again in the batter and then deep-fry, two at a time, for 30 to 45 seconds or until golden brown.
3 medium-ripe avocados, cut in wedges	
juice of 1 lemon	

cilantro sprigs	Garnish with cilantro sprigs and serve immediately with fresh salsa.
salsa, preferably quite picante	cilantro sprigs
	salsa, preferably quite picante

VARIATION

If using them as a side dish or for an interesting variation, sprinkle the freshly fried avocados with finely grated Parmesan cheese just prior to serving.

STORAGE, FREEZING, AND
ADVANCE PREPARATION

The seasoning salt, seasoned flour, and batter may be made in advance. However, for best results, fry the avocados just before serving.

MEXICAN LAYERED DIP

This popular layered appetizer is always the first to disappear. Simple to prepare and perfect to take to a party.

3   avocados
1   clove garlic, minced
2   tablespoons fresh lemon juice
1   teaspoon salt
    white pepper to taste

With a fork, mash the avocados with garlic and lemon juice, and then season with salt and white pepper. Spread half in a 9-inch pie pan.

1   small yellow onion, chopped
2   tomatoes, chopped
1   cup (about 4 ounces) grated Cheddar cheese

Top with onion, tomatoes, and cheese, then with the remaining avocado.

½   cup cooked chile con carne
¾   cup refried beans

Combine and heat the chile and beans and then add atop the avocado.

1   cup sour cream
1   cup green chiles (optional)
1   cup (about 4 ounces) grated Monterey jack cheese

Spoon the sour cream and green chiles, if desired, over the bean mixture. Top with Monterey jack cheese.

    nacho chips

Serve at room temperature with nacho chips.

STORAGE, FREEZING, AND ADVANCE PREPARATION

You may make this ahead by preparing all the ingredients early in the day and assembling the dish about 1 hour before serving.

LA FOGATA'S CHILE STRIPS
LA FOGATA'S RAJAS

Positively, this is the best appetizer anywhere, anytime. It is also good as a sauce for chicken or fish.

6   poblano chiles, roasted and peeled

Stem and seed the chiles and cut into narrow strips.

1   onion, halved and cut in strips
2–3 tablespoons vegetable oil
8   ounces cream cheese, cut in 4–5 pieces
½   teaspoon garlic powder
     pinch of ground cumin
     salt to taste
6–8 ounces Oaxaca or mozzarella cheese, grated

Sauté the onion in vegetable oil until soft and translucent, about 5 to 8 minutes. Do not brown. Add the chiles and cook 1 minute, then add the cream cheese and spices. When the cream cheese is completely melted, add the grated Oaxaca or mozzarella cheese in 6 to 8 handfuls. Allow the cheese to melt without stirring and take care to keep the temperature low.

ASSEMBLY

6–8 hot flour tortillas

Serve in individual ramekins with a hot flour tortilla draped over the top of each bowl. To eat, the raja mixture is simply spooned into the tortilla, which is rolled or folded to keep the mixture from spilling out. Remember the trick of tipping one end up so you don't lose any of the delicious filling.

STORAGE, FREEZING, AND ADVANCE PREPARATION

The chile and onion mixture may be prepared up to 2 days in advance and either refrigerated or frozen until ready to use. Be sure to reheat it before adding the two cheeses.

CRABMEAT NACHOS

Ernesto uses snow crab in his restaurant, but he says nachos made with lump crabmeat are very special. The smooth and creamy butter sauce has become his specialty. Carefully follow the directions, and never allow the butter to simmer or lose its creamy look.

2 scallions, thinly sliced 1 clove garlic, minced 1 stick unsalted butter, at room temperature 1 large tomato, peeled and chopped 1 serrano chile, minced 1 tablespoon cilantro, snipped	In a medium-size to small skillet, sauté the scallions and garlic in 1 tablespoon butter until softened. Do not allow the butter to brown. Then stir in the tomato, chile, and cilantro. Reduce the heat to low and, about 1 tablespoon at a time, whisk in the rest of the softened butter. Whisk until creamy; do not allow the butter to simmer at any time. Lift the pan from the heat if necessary to control the temperature. You may hold the sauce over a pan of hot water until ready to use.
1¾ cups cooked crabmeat ¼ cup dry sherry or vermouth	Heat the crabmeat in sherry or vermouth for a few seconds. Stir in about 1 cup of the prepared sauce and then set aside.

ASSEMBLY AND PRESENTATION

20 nacho chips 8 ounces Monterey jack cheese, grated	To assemble, place crabmeat mixture on each nacho and cover with cheese. Place 4 to 6 inches from the broiler for 3 to 5 minutes or until the cheese is melted.
1 avocado, diced 20 slices jalapeño chiles (optional)	Garnish with a few pieces of diced avocado and, if desired, a jalapeño slice.

VARIATION — You may add a cooked and halved shrimp to each nacho if desired.

STORAGE, FREEZING, AND ADVANCE PREPARATION — The sauce may be prepared in advance and held over hot water (off the heat) for about an hour.

HIGHLAND PARK NACHOS

Practically every restaurant in Texas has a version of these "Nachos Ranche-ros"; however, these are particularly interesting because of the jalapeño relish.

2   cups leftover beef, cooked and chopped, or skirt steak, char-coal-grilled and cut in bite-size pieces

Warm the meat, or if using leftover steak, place under the broiler a few minutes to heat.

1   4-ounce can jalapeño chiles, packed with carrots and onions
1   large tomato, peeled and finely chopped
2   tablespoons cilantro, minced

Strain the carrots and onions from the jalapeños and then stem and seed the chiles. Finely chop all the vegetables, then combine with the tomato and cilantro.

ASSEMBLY AND PRESENTATION

1   dozen nacho chips, preferably flat triangles
½–1 cup refried beans
1   cup Cheddar cheese, grated
1   cup Guacamole (see p. 112)
½   cup sour cream

Place the chips on an ovenproof plat-ter. Spread each chip with 1–2 tea-spoons beans. Cover the chips com-pletely with grated cheese, so that there are no chips showing through the beans and cheese. Put the chips under the broiler until the cheese melts.

Remove from oven and cover with 1–2 teaspoons Guacamole, a dollop of sour cream, 1–2 teaspoons of the relish, and then pieces of skirt steak or leftover beef.

STORAGE, FREEZING, AND ADVANCE PREPARATION

All the ingredients may be prepared in advance; however, the assembly and baking should be done just prior to serving.

CHICKEN OR SHRIMP NACHOS

1   recipe Chile and Cilantro Pesto
     (see p. 42)
3–4 tablespoons sour cream
3   dozen nacho chips
2   cups shredded cooked shrimp
     or chicken
6   ounces Monterey jack cheese,
     grated

Combine the pesto and sour cream. Spread the chips in a single layer on a cookie sheet. Top each one with a layer of the pesto, followed by shredded shrimp or chicken and finally cheese.

Place 4 to 6 inches from the broiling element for 5 to 8 minutes or until the cheese is melted and the nachos are hot.

PRESENTATION

2   tomatoes, finely diced, and/or
     sour cream

Garnish with tomatoes and/or sour cream.

STORAGE, FREEZING, AND
ADVANCE PREPARATION

The pesto may be made up to 1½ weeks ahead and the nachos assembled for baking 2 hours before you are ready to heat and serve them. Preheating the cookie sheet will insure a crisp nacho.

SEAFOOD CHEESE
QUESO DEL MAR

2	tablespoons onion, chopped
1	strip bacon, cut in several pieces

In a large skillet that may be transferred to the oven, sauté the onion and bacon until the bacon is lightly browned, about 5 to 6 minutes. Pour off excess fat.

1	medium-size tomato, peeled and chopped
¼	teaspoon garlic powder
	dash of black pepper

Add the tomato and spices to the onion mixture.

4	jumbo cooked shrimp, peeled and deveined, coarsely chopped

Add the shrimp and simmer for 1 to 2 minutes.

8	ounces Monterey jack cheese, grated, at room temperature

Add the grated cheese to the skillet, tossing to combine. Immediately transfer to a preheated 350-degree oven and bake for 3 to 5 minutes or until the cheese is melted. Stir briefly with a spoon to insure that the vegetables and shrimp are evenly distributed throughout the cheese. Take care to watch the heat and do not stir except very briefly or the cheese will clump together.

If using a microwave oven, combine the grated cheese with the shrimp and vegetables and place in a dish. Microwave on high for 1 minute or until the cheese is melted.

ASSEMBLY

4	hot flour or corn tortillas

To serve, place 2 tablespoons of the shrimp-cheese mixture in each tortilla and roll it up like a flute, turning the end up to prevent the filling from escaping.

STORAGE, FREEZING, AND ADVANCE PREPARATION

This is best when made just prior to serving.

HAM AND CHEESE

This may be used as an appetizer or a sandwich. Both standard oven and microwave instructions are given.

2 tablespoons onion, chopped 1 tablespoon butter	In a large skillet that may be transferred to the oven, sauté the onion in butter for 3−5 minutes or until translucent.
1 jalapeño chile, chopped 4 ounces cooked ham, diced ¼ teaspoon garlic powder dash of black pepper 1 medium-size tomato, peeled and chopped	Stem and seed the jalapeño and then add to onion mixture along with the ham, spices, and tomato.
8 ounces Monterey jack cheese, grated, at room temperature	Add the grated cheese to the skillet, tossing to combine. Transfer to a preheated 350-degree oven and bake 3 to 5 minutes or until the cheese is melted. Stir briefly with a spoon to insure that the vegetables and ham are evenly distributed throughout the cheese, but take care not to cook over high heat or overstir. If using a microwave oven, combine the grated cheese with the ham and vegetables and place in a dish. Microwave on high for 1 minute or until the cheese is melted.

ASSEMBLY

6 hot flour or corn tortillas	To serve, spoon into hot flour or corn tortillas. Roll up to enclose the filling, turning the end up to prevent it from escaping.
STORAGE, FREEZING, AND ADVANCE PREPARATION	This is best when made just before serving.

CHIHUAHUA CHEESE
QUESO CHIHUAHUA

This cheese may be prepared in a skillet or, if you prefer, in a microwave oven. Both instructions are given.

2   strips bacon, cut in 6 pieces
2   tablespoons   white   onion, chopped
½   small to medium-size poblano chile, roasted, peeled, and cut in strips

In a skillet that may be transferred to the oven, fry the bacon until crisp. Add the onion and poblano chile strips, and sauté 2 minutes.

8   ounces Monterey jack cheese, grated, at room temperature

Remove from heat, add the cheese, and toss to combine. Do not overstir or continue cooking. Transfer to a preheated 350-degree oven for 3 to 5 minutes or until the cheese melts.

If using a microwave oven, sprinkle the cheese over a shallow dish and then add the onion, chile, and bacon mixture. Microwave 1 minute on high.

dash of paprika

Remove from oven and sprinkle with paprika before serving.

ASSEMBLY

4   hot flour or corn tortillas, preferably fresh

To serve, place about 2 tablespoons of the mixture on a hot flour or corn tortilla and roll it up like a flute.

STORAGE, FREEZING, AND ADVANCE PREPARATION

This is best when made just prior to serving.

Soups

SOUPS

El Mirador's Mexican Soup   El Mirador
Tortilla Soup   The Mansion on Turtle Creek
Friday's Bean Soup   El Mirador
Beef Soup   El Mirador
Pumpkin Soup with Spiced Peanuts   Author's Contribution
Corn Soup   Cafe Cancún
Vermicelli Soup   El Mirador
Drunken Black Bean Soup   Cappy's

EL MIRADOR'S MEXICAN SOUP

This is the soup that brings crowds to El Mirador each weekend. Mary begins her preparation 2 days in advance.

THE STOCK

2½	quarts water
5	cloves garlic
3	fresh oregano sprigs
2	whole cloves
1	tablespoon salt
1	tablespoon ground cumin
1	teaspoon pepper
3	bay leaves, broken
1–2	basil sprigs (omit if fresh basil is not available)
5	chicken bouillon cubes
1	3-pound frying chicken, cut up

Bring the water to a boil, and then add all the ingredients, including the chicken. Skim the foam from the top as the soup simmers for 1 to 1½ hours. Remove the chicken, debone it, and shred the meat when cool. Then, strain the stock and chill. This hardens the fat for easy removal.

THE VEGETABLES

	juice of 2 limes
1	medium-size zucchini, chopped
1	yellow onion, sliced
2	stalks celery, chopped
1	carrot, chopped
1	green bell pepper, seeded and chopped
1	17-ounce can garbanzo beans, drained

The day you plan to serve the soup, reheat the defatted stock and add the juice of 2 limes. Add the vegetables and cook just until tender-crisp, about 20 minutes. Add the shredded chicken and garbanzo beans.

PRESENTATION

	Mexican Rice (see p. 126) (optional)
2	avocados, sliced
	Tila's Red Sauce (see p. 37)

To serve the soup, ladle into large soup bowls (over the rice, if using). Garnish with sliced avocados and fresh salsa.

STORAGE, FREEZING, AND ADVANCE PREPARATION

The stock may be made 1 to 2 days ahead.

TORTILLA SOUP
SOPA DE TORTILLA CHIQUITA

While there is nothing Mexican American about the Mansion, it was the first elegant restaurant to incorporate "Texas" items or offer traditional Mexican American or Southwestern specialties. The soup is an adaptation of the tortilla soup served at the Argyle Club in San Antonio. The Mansion's upscale presentation of Texas food has encouraged others to do the same, and the result will be more Southwestern specialties in fine Dallas restaurants.

3   corn tortillas
     vegetable oil or peanut oil for frying
     salt to taste

Cut the tortillas in julienne strips. Heat about 3 inches of oil to 375 to 400 degrees. Fry the tortilla strips a few at a time for about 45 seconds or until crisp. Drain on paper towels and add salt to taste. Set aside.

1   1-pound can tomatoes, coarsely chopped, including juice
2   cloves garlic
½   cup onion, chopped
1–2 tablespoons corn oil
8   cups chicken stock
1   teaspoon, more or less, ground cumin
1   teaspoon white pepper
     salt to taste
3–4 tablespoons tomato sauce, if needed

In a blender, puree the tomatoes with the garlic and onion. Transfer to a 3-quart saucepan and sauté in hot oil for 5 to 10 minutes. Add chicken stock and seasonings and simmer, uncovered, for 30 to 45 minutes or until reduced and flavorful. Adjust seasonings to taste, adding tomato sauce and more cumin if desired.

ASSEMBLY AND
PRESENTATION

1   avocado, diced
8   ounces Cheddar cheese, grated
     shredded chicken (optional)

When ready to serve, reheat the broth. Place the garnishes in small bowls to be served with the soup.

VARIATION

I like to use a combination of cheeses: a white goat cheese and Monterey jack cheese. I also find that the addition of fine-slivered white chicken and fresh basil (or cilantro) enhances this most interesting soup.

STORAGE, FREEZING, AND ADVANCE PREPARATION

The stock may be made several days in advance and, if desired, frozen.

FRIDAY'S BEAN SOUP
SOPA TARASCA

This soup gets its name from the Michoacán Indians in Mexico, who lived near the famous lake and used butterfly nets for fishing. Sopa Tarasca is a good way to use leftover beans that tastes anything but leftover.

THE BEAN BROTH

3½–4 cups whole pinto beans, in-
　　 cluding juice
2　 14½-ounce cans chicken or beef
　　 stock
1　 teaspoon salt or to taste

Combine the beans with stock and salt to taste. Bring to a simmer, using a 2½-quart saucepan, and then reduce heat and keep warm while preparing the salsa vegetables.

THE SALSA VEGETABLES

1–2 tablespoons vegetable oil
5–6 tomatoes, quartered
4　 cloves garlic, minced
1　 medium-size onion, diced
2–3 chile ancho or pasilla pods,
　　 stemmed and seeded
　　 pinch of cumin
　　 salt and pepper to taste
2　 bay leaves

Put 1–2 tablespoons of vegetable oil in a heavy-duty skillet large enough to hold the tomatoes, garlic, onion, and chile pods. Season with the cumin, salt, and pepper. Cook over medium to medium-low heat 20 to 25 minutes or until the onions and tomatoes are very soft. When the salsa vegetables are tender, puree the mixture in a blender. Then cook the salsa mixture with the bay leaves for just a few minutes, using the same skillet. Discard the bay leaves. Add this mixture to the bean broth and adjust seasonings to taste. The soup is not extremely thick—thin with additional stock if necessary and taste to adjust seasonings.

ASSEMBLY AND PRESENTATION

1　 dozen tortillas, preferably fresh
　　 peanut oil for frying

Cut the tortillas in narrow strips and spread on a cookie sheet to dry out. Deep-fry in several batches until crisp. If the strips do not dry out before frying, they tend to foam up; therefore, small batches are recommended.

4–6 ounces Monterey jack cheese, grated
1 tablespoon sour cream per serving

In a serving bowl, place a few tortilla strips and some cheese, and then cover with the soup. Garnish with sour cream dollops.

VARIATION

I like to add minced cilantro and crumbled bacon, making a ranchero-style bean soup. Canned ranch-style beans may be substituted for fresh-cooked pintos.

STORAGE, FREEZING, AND ADVANCE PREPARATION

Both the tortilla strips and the salsa vegetables may be made in advance; then you can make soup using left-over beans or have a quick, hearty meal using canned beans.

BEEF SOUP
CALDO DE RES

This is a hearty soup, typical of the northern Mexican style. It is not highly seasoned, as it is meant to be served with fresh salsas, the salt and pepper of Texas tables.

THE MEAT BROTH

1½ quarts water
1   14½-ounce can beef stock
½–1 pound beef brisket, cut in 2–3 pieces
2   beef shanks (about ¼ pound)
2   cloves garlic, minced
½   teaspoon ground cumin

Bring the water and beef stock to a boil. Add beef and return to a boil. Skim the foam that rises to the top and discard. Add the garlic and cumin, and simmer 1½ to 2 hours. When the beef is tender, remove the meat from the bones; discard the bones and fat. Skim all visible fat; this is easier to do when the soup is chilled. Place the soup in the freezer for 1 hour, then the fat is easily removed. Coarsely shred all the meat and set aside.

THE VEGETABLES

2   carrots, cut in matchstick strips
1   turnip, cut in matchstick strips
1   small onion, thinly sliced
1   bell pepper, cut in matchstick strips
⅓   head green cabbage, thinly sliced
2   stalks celery, cut in matchstick strips
1   zucchini, cut in matchstick strips
5–6 cilantro sprigs and/or 3 mint sprigs
     salt and pepper to taste

Cut the vegetables of your choice into matchstick strips, 2½ by ¼ inches. Return the broth to a boil and add the shredded meat, carrots, turnip, onion, and bell pepper. Cook 5 to 6 minutes. After a few minutes, add the remaining vegetables and the herbs of your choice. Adjust seasonings. Cook just long enough to make all the vegetables tender-crisp, about 2 more minutes.

EL MIRADOR

ASSEMBLY AND PRESENTATION

6   *corn tortillas*
      peanut oil for frying
      salt
      Tila's Red Sauce (see p. 37)
      Green Chile Salsa (see p. 39)
      Pico de Gallo (see p. 40)

Cut the tortillas into thin julienne strips and deep-fry in several batches until crisp. If the oil foams, you have fried too many at one time—either air-dry the strips 2 to 3 hours to remove moisture or fry in smaller batches.

Lightly salt and serve with the soup along with salsas.

STORAGE, FREEZING, AND ADVANCE PREPARATION

The broth may be prepared a day in advance. Adjust salt and pepper in the soup when reheating.

PUMPKIN SOUP WITH SPICED PEANUTS

This soup is as good chilled as it is hot.

1½   *pounds fresh pumpkin, peeled, seeds and strings removed, or equal amounts cooked and pureed winter squash (acorn or butternut) and canned pumpkin*
½   *stick unsalted butter*
1   *tablespoon flour*

In a medium-size saucepan, cook the fresh pumpkin until very tender, about 15 to 20 minutes. In a blender, puree the pumpkin along with the butter and flour. If using winter squash, peel, seed, and cook the same way.

2   *14½-ounce cans chicken stock*
½   *cup whole milk*

Bring the chicken stock and milk to a boil. Stir in the pumpkin and winter squash, if using, and return to a boil. Reduce heat immediately. Blend again if you want a smoother soup.

1   *cup heavy cream*
1½   *teaspoons salt*
¼   *teaspoon white pepper*
      cayenne pepper to taste

Stir in the cream and then season with salt, pepper, and cayenne. Allow the soup to simmer and thicken for 30 to 40 minutes, stirring occasionally. Keep warm until ready to serve or refrigerate and serve when chilled.

PRESENTATION

    spiced hot peanuts or roasted and salted pumpkin seeds
    minced cilantro

Garnish the hot or cold soup with spiced peanuts or pumpkin seeds and minced cilantro. Spiced hot peanuts are available in many stores that carry specialty Mexican foods.

STORAGE, FREEZING, AND ADVANCE PREPARATION

The soup may be made 1 to 2 days in advance. It freezes well; however, it may need vigorous whisking when thawed.

CORN SOUP

This delicious soup tends to vary in thickness. Simply thin with milk or water to your preference.

2	tablespoons cornstarch
6–8	cups whole milk

Dissolve the cornstarch in 1 cup of the milk and set aside.

1	medium-size onion, peeled and chopped
1	clove garlic, minced
1½	sticks unsalted butter (do not use margarine)
2	teaspoons chile powder
2	teaspoons ground cumin
1	teaspoon garlic powder
½	teaspoon black pepper
1–1½	teaspoons salt or to taste
4	cups fresh or frozen corn
½	cup masa harina
3–4	green chiles, chopped

In a large saucepan or soup pot, sauté the onion and garlic in butter until soft and translucent, about 8 to 10 minutes. Add spices and stir to dissolve them. Add the corn and then transfer to a blender or food processor. Turn the machine on and, while it is running, add the reserved 1 cup milk. Return to medium heat and add masa harina and the remaining milk, stirring occasionally. Add the green chiles and cook for 10 to 15 minutes. Adjust salt to taste.

PRESENTATION

8	ounces Monterey jack cheese, grated

To serve, pour the hot soup into oven-proof serving bowls. Top with grated cheese and heat in the oven just long enough to melt the cheese. Do not brown.

1	cup picante sauce or Pico de Gallo (see p. 40) nacho chips

Garnish with your favorite picante sauce or Pico de Gallo. Serve with chips.

STORAGE, FREEZING, AND ADVANCE PREPARATION

This soup may be made a day in advance, and it freezes well. When reheating, do not allow it to cook for a long period of time or it may become too thick.

VERMICELLI SOUP
SOPA DE FIDEO

This is actually more of a side dish than a soup. The addition of 3 to 4 more cups of chicken or beef stock will make a more souplike consistency. I urge you to add seasoned chorizo or East Texas sausage, as described in the variation. This is a mildly seasoned dish which is easily spiced, if desired, with minced jalapeño.

8 ounces vermicelli, broken in small pieces 2–3 tablespoons oil, heated	In a large skillet, over medium heat, sauté the vermicelli in hot oil. Watch carefully since it burns easily; however, be sure all the pieces are browned.
4 tomatoes, cores intact 1 yellow onion, cut in 4–5 pieces 2 cloves garlic, unpeeled	Place the tomatoes, onion, and garlic on an oiled cookie sheet 4 inches from the broiling element. Leave the door ajar and cook until charred and caramelized. Cool and peel the garlic, and then puree the vegetables and all their juices in a blender.
2 cups, more or less, chicken stock, preferably homemade	Immediately add the blended tomato, onion, and garlic mixture to the vermicelli with enough stock to achieve a soupy consistency.
1 bunch green onions, chopped 1 clove garlic, minced 2 tablespoons vegetable oil 2 bell peppers, chopped or sliced (use red or green peppers or a combination of both) ½ cup cilantro leaves, snipped, or 2 mint sprigs salt and pepper to taste	In a separate skillet, sauté the onions and garlic in oil 2 minutes. Stir in the peppers and cilantro or mint and adjust liquid as necessary. Add salt and pepper to taste. Add the onion-pepper mixture to the vermicelli.

PRESENTATION

2–3 ounces Parmesan cheese, grated	Serve garnished with Parmesan cheese.

EL MIRADOR

VARIATION

This soup may be served like a one-dish stew by adding cooked chicken pieces (preferably thighs), a cooked seasoned chorizo-style sausage, or East Texas sausage. Sauté your choice of fowl or meat and then serve atop each portion. Garnish with fresh cilantro. You may substitute 1 14½-ounce or 1-pound can Italian-style tomatoes, if desired. Sauté with the onions and garlic to brown in place of roasting in the oven.

STORAGE, FREEZING, AND ADVANCE PREPARATION

This dish may be made ahead and reheated quite successfully. You will need to add more stock when reheating, as the pasta absorbs the liquid. Be sure to adjust seasonings.

DRUNKEN BLACK BEAN SOUP

I like to serve this soup for a winter brunch along with eggs scrambled with tostados and salsa, fresh fruit, and Mexican sweet rolls.

1 *pound dried black beans* 9–10 *cups chicken stock*	Wash, drain, and pick through beans to remove stones and/or spoiled beans. In a large stockpot, bring the chicken stock and beans to a boil.
¼ *pound bacon, chopped* 1 *onion, diced* 1 *clove garlic, minced*	In a medium-size skillet or sauté pan, sauté the bacon with onion and garlic, until the bacon is lightly browned. Add to the beans and cook over medium heat about an hour, or until the beans are just tender and the stock has thickened.
2–3 *tablespoons tomato paste* ½–1 *teaspoon salt* ¼–½ *teaspoon pepper*	Add the tomato paste, salt, and pepper, being careful not to get the soup too salty. Adjust seasonings to taste as necessary.
½–1 *tablespoon cilantro, minced* 1 *cup beer*	Stir in cilantro and beer and continue cooking 1 to 1½ hours. The soup should have an abundant amount of broth; be prepared to add more chicken stock if necessary.

PRESENTATION

8–12 *ounces Monterey jack cheese,* *grated*	To serve, place about ½ cup beans in a soup bowl. Add about 1 ounce of cheese per serving. Spoon additional broth on top.
cilantro sprigs (optional) 8–12 *radishes, sliced (optional)*	Garnish with cilantro or sliced radishes if desired.

STORAGE, FREEZING, AND ADVANCE PREPARATION

You may prepare this soup several days in advance; however, the beans may absorb the broth and more stock may be needed.

Salads

SALADS

Lydia's Southwestern Apple Salad	Cappy's
Joaquín Salad	Las Canarias
Fruit Salad	Author's Contribution
Vegetable Salad	El Mirador
Nopalito Salad	El Mirador
Warm Vegetable Salad	El Mirador
Sangría Mousse	Bennie Ferrell Catering
Guacamole Salad	Tila's

LYDIA'S SOUTHWESTERN APPLE SALAD

This salad is the inspiration of one of Cappy's chief cooks. It is a perfect accompaniment for grilled entrées, chile con carne, or beef stew.

THE DRESSING

½   cup mayonnaise
¼   cup sour cream
½   teaspoon dried dill weed or 1 teaspoon fresh dill, snipped
¼ ½ teaspoon ground cumin or to taste

Stir the ingredients together to make a smooth dressing.

THE SALAD

3–4   apples, cut in bite-size pieces
      juice of 1 lime
½   cup seedless raisins
6   stalks celery, cut in bite-size pieces
1   11-ounce can mandarin oranges, drained

      lettuce or cabbage leaves

Core but do not peel the apples and then cut as directed. Toss in lime juice to coat all exposed surfaces and retard browning. Combine with raisins, celery, and dressing. Mix until coated with dressing and then fold in the oranges.

Serve on fresh lettuce leaves or in a large, crisp cabbage leaf.

STORAGE, FREEZING, AND ADVANCE PREPARATION

The salad may be prepared several hours in advance, omitting only the apples. Add apples just prior to serving.

JOAQUÍN SALAD

A beautiful and elegant salad.

THE DRESSING

1	cup heavy mayonnaise
½	cup honey
	juice of 1 lime
1	ounce green crème de menthe

In a blender or a food processor fitted with a metal blade, process the dressing ingredients until smooth. Set aside or refrigerate until ready to use.

THE SALAD

½	head iceberg lettuce, finely shredded
2–3	avocados, sliced
20	grapefruit sections, more or less, preferably pink
4	large fresh strawberries

Divide the lettuce among 4 salad plates. Cover with alternating rows of avocado and grapefruit sections, using about 5 slices of each per salad. Place a whole strawberry on top. Then drizzle with the dressing.

VARIATION

I prefer a sweet leaf lettuce such as Boston or Bibb for this salad. When pomegranates are in season, garnish the salad with pomegranate seeds. In this case, slice the strawberries and alternate with avocado and grapefruit sections.

STORAGE, FREEZING, AND ADVANCE PREPARATION

The dressing may be prepared a day in advance; however, the avocados should be sliced just prior to serving.

FRUIT SALAD

Vinaigrette dressings are surprisingly good with many fruits as well as vegetables for an interesting and refreshing salad to accompany both tortilla specialties or grilled entrées. This salad pairs well with brunch dishes from egg-and-bacon tacos to your favorite huevos rancheros.

THE DRESSING

3	*tablespoons white wine vinegar*
2	*tablespoons fresh orange or grapefruit juice*
½	*cup safflower oil*
1	*shallot, finely minced*
½	*teaspoon salt*
¼	*teaspoon dry mustard*
	pinch of white pepper

In a blender or a food processor fitted with a metal blade, combine the dressing ingredients and set aside.

THE SALAD

1	*head Bibb lettuce*
2	*cups (about 4 grapefruits) pink grapefruit sections*
2	*papayas, sliced*
1	*cup fresh berries, preferably* raspberries *or* thickly sliced strawberries
2	*avocados, sliced*

Mist the lettuce to clean and wipe dry. Line 4 cold salad plates with lettuce leaves. Arrange the fruits and avocado sections on the lettuce, with the berries placed at random. Drizzle with dressing just prior to serving.

STORAGE, FREEZING, AND ADVANCE PREPARATION

All the fruits, except the avocados, may be sliced about 2 hours ahead. Do not add the dressing or arrange the salad until serving time, as the fruits will lose their crisp texture and may become mushy.

VEGETABLE SALAD
ENSALADA DE VERDURAS

Mary's vegetables have a distinctive look, as she likes a julienne cut rather than a more typical diced or cubed cut. I suggest a short julienne, about ¼ inch by 1 inch. This versatile potato salad is good with the mayonnaise dressing given, or, if you prefer, use your favorite hot bacon dressing and garnish the plates with fresh spinach. The salad is perfect with grilled fish.

THE DRESSING

½	*cup mayonnaise*
1	*tablespoon safflower oil*
2	*tablespoons wine vinegar*
1	*tablespoon prepared mustard*
¼	*cup heavy cream* or *sour cream*

Combine the dressing ingredients, adjusting the seasoning to taste. The cream adds smoothness to both taste and texture.

THE SALAD

6–8	*small red potatoes*
2	*carrots, peeled*
3	*stalks celery*
1	*small red bell pepper, seeded and cut in strips*
½	*green bell pepper, seeded and cut in strips*

Boil the potatoes, in their skins, with enough water to cover, until tender. Cool and then cut them in pieces about ¼ to ½ by 1 inch. Drain and cool.

In the same pan, boil the carrots in lightly salted water until tender-crisp. Remove with tongs and then blanch celery for 30 seconds.

Cool both carrots and celery and cut in the same size pieces as the potatoes. Gently toss all the vegetables together with the dressing, taking care not to break up the potatoes.

minced fresh cilantro or *parsley*

Garnish with minced cilantro or parsley.

EL MIRADOR

VARIATION

I like narrow strips of both red bell pepper (not pimiento) and a mild green chile, roasted and peeled, in this salad. A garnish of either capers, chopped egg, or sliced black olives is most attractive.

STORAGE, FREEZING, AND ADVANCE PREPARATION

The entire salad may be prepared up to a day ahead; it keeps quite well.

NOPALITO SALAD

The nopal cactus, also known as prickly pear, is sold in cans in many groceries. Mary Treviño calls this a very basic Mexican salad. You may use green peas or green beans if jícama is not available.

THE DRESSING

½	*teaspoon salt* or *to taste*
¼	*teaspoon pepper*
½	*teaspoon dry mustard*
¼	*cup vinegar*
½	*cup oil*
¼	*teaspoon leaf oregano*
½	*cup sour cream*

Whisk or blend the dressing ingredients vigorously to combine. Adjust seasonings to taste.

THE SALAD

1	*small yellow onion, halved and cut in strips*
1½	*cups canned nopal cactus, chopped*
1	*3-ounce jar pimientos, rinsed, or 2 bell peppers, diced*
2	*cups jícama, chopped*

Place the onions in a colander. Pour about 1 quart boiling water over them. This removes the raw taste and leaves the onions crisp. Rinse immediately with cold water and let stand.

Toss together the onions, cactus, pimientos or red bell peppers, and jícama. Toss the dressing and salad together just prior to serving.

ASSEMBLY AND PRESENTATION

1	*cup sautéed chopped walnuts* or *pine nuts* *Boston lettuce leaves*

Sauté the walnuts, if using, for 2 to 3 minutes, then drain on paper towels.

Place the salad on a lettuce leaf. Garnish with walnuts or pine nuts.

WARM VEGETABLE SALAD

Mary Treviño describes her salads as simple but traditional. This one may be served hot, just after sautéing, with butter and minced cilantro, or cold with a vinaigrette dressing.

THE DRESSING

1	clove garlic
9	tablespoons oil
3	tablespoons vinegar
½–1	teaspoon salt
¼	teaspoon pepper
¼	cup crisp-cooked bacon (optional)
	snipped cilantro (optional)

In a blender or a food processor fitted with a metal blade, process the garlic and other ingredients until smooth and well combined. Add snipped cilantro, if desired. Set aside, at room temperature, until ready to use.

THE SALAD

1	onion, thinly sliced in rings
1–2	tablespoons oil
2	zucchini, sliced
1	crookneck squash, sliced, or any combination of squashes romaine or Boston lettuce leaves

In a large skillet or sauté pan, sauté the onion in oil until soft and translucent. Then toss in the squashes and sauté briefly to cook tender-crisp. Transfer while warm to salad plates lined with crisp romaine or Boston lettuce leaves.

PRESENTATION

Monterey jack cheese, grated, or warm, herbed goat cheese

Heat the dressing just before drizzling atop the salad. Do not boil. Top with cheese.

SANGRÍA MOUSSE

This attractive dish may be used as a dessert or a salad—it is a delightful accompaniment to assertive entrées.

12	*individual 1-cup molds* or *1 angel food cake pan* or *bundt pan*

Prepare the molds by rinsing them with cold water.

CLEAR LAYER

2	*tablespoons unflavored gelatin*
1	*cup cold water*
¼	*cup sugar*
⅔	*cup (1 6-ounce can) frozen lemonade concentrate*
1	*cup cold water*
½	*cup White Wine Sangría (see p. 228)*
2	*seedless oranges, peeled and sliced*

Sprinkle gelatin over cold water and let stand 5 minutes to soften. Place over moderate heat and stir constantly until gelatin dissolves, about 5 minutes. Remove from heat.

Add sugar, stirring to dissolve, then frozen lemonade concentrate, stirring to melt. Add 1 cup cold water and Sangría, and then pour the mixture into each mold and chill until almost firm. Press orange slices into the mixture and refrigerate.

CREAM LAYER

3	*tablespoons unflavored gelatin*
1	*cup cold water*
½	*cup sugar*
1⅓	*cups (1 12-ounce can) frozen lemonade concentrate*
¾	*cup cold water*
1	*cup White Wine Sangría (see p. 228)*
1	*cup heavy cream*

Sprinkle gelatin over cold water and let stand 5 minutes to soften. Place over moderate heat and stir constantly until gelatin dissolves, about 5 minutes. Remove from heat.

Add sugar, stirring to dissolve, then frozen lemonade concentrate, stirring to melt. Add ¾ cup cold water and Sangría. Chill until mixture is the consistency of unbeaten egg white.

Whip heavy cream until stiff and then fold into the chilled mixture until very smooth. Pour over the chilled clear layer. Chill until firm.

BENNIE FERRELL

PRESENTATION

*1   quart   fresh   strawberries,
      halved,* or *other fresh fruit*

Unmold onto a serving platter and garnish with fresh strawberries or fresh fruit of your choice.

STORAGE, FREEZING, AND ADVANCE PREPARATION

This may be made a day in advance and refrigerated, covered loosely, until ready to serve. Garnish at serving time.

GUACAMOLE SALAD

Clive Duval uses this basic recipe for his Guacamole Salad. The texture and taste are simple but perfect, and I find it excellent as a relish or filling as well. The presentation is for a salad; however, feel free to utilize this in your own manner.

6   *medium-ripe avocados, coarsely chopped*

1   *cup fresh lime juice*

2½—3 *cups Pico de Gallo (see p. 40)*
        salt and pepper to taste

Roughly cut up the avocados into large chunks and then combine with lime juice. Gently toss with Pico de Gallo and then season to taste with salt and pepper.

Refrigerate until ready to use. The lime juice and the Pico de Gallo will help retard browning.

PRESENTATION

romaine or *Boston lettuce leaves*
nacho chips

Serve on lettuce leaves with chips.

STORAGE, FREEZING, AND ADVANCE PREPARATION

The Pico de Gallo may be made 2 to 3 hours ahead. If the Pico de Gallo is made with tomatilloes, the Guacamole may also be made earlier without significant browning.

FROM CAPPY LAWTON

To prepare avocado slices in advance and prevent darkening, try the following. Have ready a misting bottle filled with two parts lemon juice to one part water. Lay avocado slices atop waxed paper. Mist with lemon juice, then cover with another sheet of waxed paper.

FROM MARIANO MARTÍNEZ

When storing guacamole, do not stir it even if a dark film coats the top. Simply skim it and discard before serving. You'll be surprised how fresh the guacamole is under this dark film.

FROM ERNESTO TORRES

The addition of cream or half-and-half to guacamole will enhance the flavor as well as help retard darkening.

AUTHOR'S CONTRIBUTION

In each guacamole recipe calling for 3 avocados, you may substitute 2 fresh tomatilloes, finely minced, for the lemon juice. This helps keep the bright green color better than any method I've tried and has a cleaner citrus taste than the lemon.

Always whisk in lemon juice just prior to serving for all avocado sauces, relishes, or soups. If lemon is added early and then left to stand, the final result can taste bitter.

Vegetables and Accompaniments

LAS CANARIAS
Center: Roast Suckling Pig With Fruit
Garnishes, Black Beans, Rice and
Accompaniments

Far Left: Paella Levantina
Upper Far Left: Banana Capitán
Far Right: Oyster and Clam Ceviche

VEGETABLES AND ACCOMPANIMENTS

Los Tres Bobos' Fried Zucchini   Los Tres Bobos
Sautéed Squash   Author's Contribution
Tila's Chile Strips   Tila's
Aztec Corn   Author's Contribution
Julia's Beans   Julia Segovia Ramírez
Fried Potatoes   Tila's
Black Beans   Las Canarias
Mexican Rice   Cafe Cancún

LOS TRES BOBOS' FRIED ZUCCHINI

The triple-dipping technique insures a light and crisp coating. The secret to deep-frying is having the oil at the proper temperature; use a thermometer to be sure.

THE ZUCCHINI

7–8 zucchini	Cut the zucchini in sticks 2 to 3 inches in length.

THE DRY BATTER

3 *cups flour* 1 *cup biscuit mix* 2 *tablespoons salt* 1 *tablespoon black pepper* 1 *teaspoon garlic salt*	Blend ingredients until well mixed. Set aside.

THE WET BATTER

1 *egg* 2 *cups buttermilk* ½ *cup biscuit mix* 1 *cup iced water* 1 *tablespoon leaf oregano* 4 *jalapeño chiles, stemmed, seeded, and finely minced*	Blend ingredients to mix thoroughly. Set aside.

ASSEMBLY AND PRESENTATION

peanut oil for frying *minced leaf oregano (optional)* *Green Chile Cream Sauce (see p. 43) or Ernesto's Hot Sauce (see p. 41)*	Heat the oil to between 350 and 375 degrees. Dip the zucchini in the dry batter, then in the wet, and then again in the dry. Deep-fry until golden brown. Sprinkle oregano on top if desired. Serve with Los Tres Bobos' Green Chile Cream Sauce or Ernesto's Hot Sauce.

STORAGE, FREEZING, AND ADVANCE PREPARATION

The batters may be made ahead, but the vegetables are best fried just prior to serving.

SAUTÉED SQUASH

This is a colorful sauté that will accompany grilled items or enchiladas.

2 *zucchini*
2 *crookneck squash*
1 *bell pepper*

Cut both squashes into matchstick strips, about ¼ by 2½ inches, discarding seeds and pulp if heavily seeded or pulpy. Stem and seed the pepper and then cut in strips about the same size as the squashes.

1 *tablespoon vegetable oil*
½ *tablespoon unsalted butter*
   salt and coarse-ground black pepper to taste
   pinch of chile powder or *cayenne pepper*
   minced fresh herbs such as cilantro and oregano

In a large skillet or wok, heat the oil and butter. Add all the vegetables and stir-fry for 2 to 3 minutes or until tender but slightly crisp.

Season to taste as desired, tossing to be sure the vegetables are well coated.

TILA'S CHILE STRIPS
TILA'S RAJAS

These rajas in cream may be used as is with enchiladas or grilled entrées or with any of the suggested vegetables to accompany baked chicken or fish.

1½   white onions, halved and sliced
½   stick unsalted butter
6   large poblano chiles, roasted and peeled
1–2 cups heavy cream
     salt and pepper to taste

In a 10-inch skillet, sauté the onions in butter until soft and translucent, 15 to 20 minutes. Add the chiles and cream. Use the greater amount of cream if you plan to serve as a sauce for enchiladas or a grilled entrée. Simmer 5 to 8 minutes or until reduced and thickened. Season to taste.

VARIATION

You may serve this mixture as an appetizer, with flour tortillas, by using the lesser amount of cream and adding 2–3 tablespoons grated Monterey jack or Parmesan cheese. To serve with vegetables, blanch matchstick strips of zucchini, red bell pepper, and/or carrots; then add to the sautéed onions and chiles after they have cooked 5 minutes. Simmer 2–3 minutes or until the cream has thickened.

STORAGE, FREEZING, AND ADVANCE PREPARATION

The onions and chiles (and vegetables if using) may be cut and prepared ahead; however, the dish should be cooked and assembled just prior to serving.

119

AZTEC CORN

This is the perfect recipe for summer, when you are cooking outdoors. Your barbecue grill is also the perfect way to roast the peppers, giving them a wonderful flavor, but you may also cook Aztec Corn indoors.

3	*large ears fresh sweet corn, in husks, white or yellow*

Husk the corn, discarding silks and spotted husks. Soak the remaining husks for at least 30 minutes in water. Use as many husks as necessary to make 6 containers for about ¾ to 1 cup vegetables each. Then lay each one on a rectangular piece of aluminum foil, about 10 by 6 inches.

With a sharp knife, remove kernels from the cobs, taking care to use all the milky liquid.

3	*tablespoons unsalted butter*
6	*green onions, sliced*
¼	*teaspoon salt*
	pepper to taste
1	*poblano chile, roasted, peeled, and chopped,* or *1–2 canned green chiles, chopped*
1	*red bell pepper, chopped*
1	*cup chopped zucchini* or *peas (optional)*

Melt the butter in a large skillet over medium heat. Add corn, green onions, salt, and pepper. Sauté about 5 minutes, and then add chopped chiles and red pepper. If using the optional vegetables, add to the skillet with the peppers.

½	*cup salsa*
	juice of 1 lime

Stir in salsa and lime juice, and taste and adjust seasonings.

ASSEMBLY AND PRESENTATION

6	*fresh oregano* or *basil sprigs*

Spoon about ¾ to 1 cup of the vegetables into the prepared husks, spreading them flat to make an oblong, boat-shaped container. Fold the foil over the husks, pinching to secure both ends and long edges. The vegetables will be grilled in this package.

Prepare barbecue grill. Arrange husks on cooler edge of grill. Grill about 8 to 10 minutes, without turning.

AUTHOR'S CONTRIBUTION

If baking in the oven, preheat to 375 degrees and bake directly on the rack for 12 to 15 minutes.

To serve, open the foil and then slide the vegetables in their husks onto plates. Garnish with oregano or basil.

AUTHOR'S NOTE

You may enclose the vegetables completely in the husks alone, securing in the same fashion as if making tamales. Brush with water while grilling to prevent the husks from scorching. This will impart more charcoal flavor.

STORAGE, FREEZING, AND ADVANCE PREPARATION

The vegetables may be sautéed and the husks filled and sealed early in the day. Simply refrigerate until ready to grill.

JULIA SEGOVIA RAMÍREZ

JULIA'S BEANS

When Julia Segovia Ramírez moved to San Antonio in 1962, she brought with her the family traditions and recipes which had been handed down for generations. No cookbook from Texas would be complete without a recipe for beans. While the new trend is to move away from beans as an accompaniment to every dish, beans remain important, and Julia's are the best I have come across.

Julia's basic bean recipe is a staple, fairly bland dish that appears almost daily in most Mexican homes. For a spicier dish, Julia adds to the basic recipe to produce Beans a la Charra.

The Borracho Beans came from the haciendas of Mexico. The kitchens of the large ranches were pressed to provide food 24 hours a day. Often the cooks had to work through the night while the owner of the ranch and his family and other workers slept. During those nighttime hours, the cooks liked to take a little nip of beer or wine. As the story goes, on one occasion the cook got careless and spilled beer into the beans. When the owner tasted the beans the next day, he commended the cook on the new seasoning. The beans were dubbed drunken beans.

1 pound dried pinto beans 1 quart water	Soak the beans in about 1 quart hot water, just enough to thoroughly cover, for 30 minutes. Remove any hard pieces, and then rinse the beans in cool water and drain.
5–6 cups fresh water 1 teaspoon salt 2 cloves garlic, peeled 2–3 strips bacon, finely chopped (optional)	Cook the beans in 5–6 cups fresh water. After the first 30 minutes, add the salt, garlic, and bacon, if desired. Then let simmer 2 to 3 hours, watching carefully and adding water as needed. When fully cooked, adjust the salt to taste.

VARIATION: Beans a la Charra

2 serrano chiles, stemmed, seeded, and minced 2 jalapeño chiles, stemmed, seeded, and minced 1 medium-size onion, chopped 10 strips bacon, chopped and sautéed until brown 2–3 tablespoons cilantro, minced	During the last 30 minutes, add all the ingredients except the cilantro. Stir in minced cilantro just before serving.

JULIA SEGOVIA RAMIREZ

PRESENTATION

snipped cilantro
4   ounces Monterey jack cheese, grated
2–3 tomatoes, diced
1   onion, diced
     avocado slices
2–3 serrano chiles, diced

Serve with bowls of cilantro, cheese, tomatoes, onion, avocado, and chiles. Add homemade flour tortillas and you will have a good "vegetarian" buffet.

STORAGE, FREEZING, AND ADVANCE PREPARATION

Beans always taste better if they are prepared in advance and reheated.

FRIED POTATOES
PAPAS FRITAS

Although the title implies that the potatoes are fried, they are actually sautéed in a minimum of safflower oil. You will need a well-seasoned skillet or one with a nonstick surface.

3 potatoes, peeled and cut in pieces about the size of shelled walnuts 1 quart water (to cover potatoes) salt	Boil the potatoes in lightly salted water until tender, about 15 minutes. Refresh under cold water and set aside.
¼–½ pound bacon, chopped 1 white onion, chopped 2 tomatoes, cored and diced 2 jalapeño chiles, stemmed, seeded, and chopped salt and pepper to taste	In a large sauté pan or skillet, sauté the bacon until crisp. Set aside. Pour off all but about 2 tablespoons of the fat and add onion, cooking until soft and translucent, about 3 minutes. Add tomatoes and jalapeños. Season to taste. Remove and set mixture aside.
1–2 tablespoons safflower oil	Using the same skillet, add a thin coating of safflower oil and sauté the potatoes until crisp. Stir in reserved bacon and vegetables. Serve hot as an accompaniment to meat, poultry, or egg dishes.
STORAGE, FREEZING, AND ADVANCE PREPARATION	The potatoes may be cooked ahead and chilled, and the bacon mixture may be prepared ahead. Then, sauté the potatoes prior to serving.

BLACK BEANS

THE TOMATO SALSA

6	tomatoes, chopped
1	bunch cilantro, snipped
1	bunch scallions, thinly sliced
	salt and pepper to taste

No more than 3 to 4 hours before serving, combine tomatoes, cilantro, and scallions. Season to taste with salt and pepper and refrigerate.

THE MEXICAN CREAM

2	cups sour cream
1	cup heavy cream
1	teaspoon fresh lime juice

In a glass bowl, combine creams and lime juice and let stand at room temperature 2 hours. Refrigerate until ready to use.

THE BEANS

1½	cups dried black beans
10	strips bacon, chopped
2	carrots, roughly chopped
4	stalks celery, diced

Wash and sort through the black beans. In a medium-size skillet, sauté the bacon until lightly browned. Add carrots and celery and cook an additional 2 to 3 minutes. Set aside.

1	quart water
6	cups chicken stock
1	onion, chopped
2	cloves garlic, minced
2	teaspoons salt
½	teaspoon pepper
1	teaspoon ground cloves

In a large saucepan, combine the beans with water and chicken stock. Add the bacon mixture, onion, garlic, and seasonings and simmer over medium heat until the beans are tender, about 2 to 3 hours. Check and add more water if necessary to insure a rich broth. Adjust the seasonings to taste.

PRESENTATION

Serve the beans with the Mexican cream and tomato salsa. Rice may be served on the side.

STORAGE, FREEZING, AND ADVANCE PREPARATION

Beans are best made ahead of time and reheated.

MEXICAN RICE

Mexican rice is a standard accompaniment to many Mexican American specialties. Be sure to try the variation with cheese.

1 1-pound can whole tomatoes, including juice 1 cup onion, diced 1–2 serrano chiles, stemmed and seeded	Break up the tomatoes with a fork and then combine with onion and chiles.
2 cups chicken stock 1–1½ cups frozen corn 1 cup frozen peas 1 cup fresh or frozen carrots, diced ½–1 teaspoon salt or to taste ½ teaspoon garlic powder	In a large saucepan, add the tomato mixture to the chicken stock, vegetables, and seasonings. Bring to a boil and keep warm.
1 cup raw unrefined rice 1–2 tablespoons vegetable oil	In a large skillet, sauté the rice in hot oil about 5 minutes, stirring constantly until the rice turns white. Add the tomato and vegetable mixture to the rice and bring to a boil. Simmer over low heat, covered, about 13 minutes. Check after 7 to 8 minutes to see if the liquid has been absorbed. Cook until tender, 13 to 15 minutes.

PRESENTATION

minced cilantro

Serve garnished with minced cilantro.

VARIATION

When in season, 1 red bell pepper, chopped, is a delicious and colorful addition. Or stir ⅓ cup grated Parmesan cheese into the cooked rice and heat just until melted. It may be necessary to add more liquid.

STORAGE, FREEZING, AND ADVANCE PREPARATION

The rice may be made in advance and then reheated. It will be necessary to add hot water when reheating. You may freeze the rice; however, there is some loss of texture.

FROM RUBEN AND CARMELA LÓPEZ

Prevent rice from getting soggy, with the added advantage of advance preparation, by the following method. Cook the rice, reducing the cooking time 10 minutes. Refrigerate, drained, and then reheat in fresh chicken stock or hot water when you are ready to serve. If you include freshly minced vegetables, sauté these separately and add when reheating the rice.

FROM MARIANO MARTÍNEZ

When storing pinto beans, drain off the excess liquid and refrigerate beans and liquid separately. The beans will stay fresh longer. You may add chicken stock when reheating.

Tortilla Specialties

TORTILLA SPECIALTIES

Mexican Pizza	La Esquina
Quesadilla Yucatán	Cafe Cancún
Marianitos	Mariano's
Onion and Cheese Quesadillas	La Esquina
Chimichangas	La Hacienda
Gorditas	Cappy's
Chicken Chilaquiles	La Hacienda
Soft Chicken Tacos	La Fogata
Turnovers	The Tavern
Green Chicken Enchiladas	La Fogata
Ninfa's Green Enchiladas	Ninfa's
Poblano and Cheese Enchiladas	Tila's
Ninfa's Crab Enchiladas	Ninfa's
San Miguel's Crabmeat Enchiladas	Fonda San Miguel
Shrimp Enchiladas	Los Tres Bobos

MEXICAN PIZZA

This delicious layered concoction, the invention of the chefs at the Anatole, is served for Saturday brunch. It is a most colorful and satisfying dish, which may be an appetizer for 16 to 18, a brunch or lunch entrée for 12, or dinner for 6 hungry teenagers. It holds well on a warming tray and makes a spectacular buffet dish.

1 pound ground beef	In a large skillet, sauté the ground meat 5 to 8 minutes until fully cooked. Drain off all excess fat.
2 tomatoes, diced 1 onion, chopped 1 teaspoon ground cumin 1–2 teaspoons chile powder ½ teaspoon salt ¼ teaspoon pepper 1½ cups Julia's Beans (see p. 122), partially mashed	Add the tomatoes and onion to the meat and cook 3 to 5 minutes more until the onion is soft. Season the beef mixture with cumin, chile powder, salt, and pepper to taste. Stir the beans into the mixture and set aside.
1½–2 cups shredded cooked chicken (optional) 1 cup picante sauce (optional)	Mix the cooked chicken with the picante sauce, if using.
1¼ pounds Longhorn Cheddar cheese, shredded 1¼ pounds Monterey jack cheese, shredded	Divide the cheese into thirds.
2 red peppers 4 green peppers 4 jalapeño chiles, seeded 3 tomatoes	Chop the vegetables and set them aside.

ASSEMBLY AND PRESENTATION

14 12-inch burrito-size flour tortillas 2 cups sour cream butter	Use a buttered jelly roll pan with sides. Begin with 6 tortillas, covering the entire surface and overlapping the sides. Next, spread all the ground beef and bean mixture, topped with half the sour cream. Sprinkle with both the cheeses, using ⅓ the total amount. Scatter ⅓

131

of the chopped peppers and tomatoes over the cheeses. Repeat, using only 4 tortillas for the second layer. Spread with the chicken (if using), followed by the remaining sour cream, ⅓ of the cheeses, and ⅓ of the vegetables. Repeat, using the final 4 tortillas. Press the sides of the tortillas inward all around the edge of the pan to enclose filling. Top with remaining cheeses and chopped tomatoes and peppers. Brush all exposed tortilla surfaces with butter. Bake at 350 degrees about 35 to 45 minutes.

fresh parsley

Sprinkle with fresh parsley just before serving. Cut into squares to serve.

STORAGE, FREEZING, AND ADVANCE PREPARATION

The pizza may be assembled 24 hours in advance and refrigerated until ready to bake. It may be frozen for 2 to 3 months; thaw before baking.

QUESADILLA YUCATÁN

This quesadilla uses 2 corn tortillas, one layered atop the other, with cheese melted between and a zucchini sauce on top. Cafe Cancún uses Chihuahua cheese, which has a sharper, more distinctive taste than either Monterey jack or Cheddar.

1	onion, sliced
1	cup corn
¼	cup olive oil
10	zucchini, thinly sliced
1–2	tablespoons soy sauce or sauce of your choice
½	tablespoon Tabasco sauce
½	teaspoon garlic powder
	salt and pepper to taste
	chile powder to taste
2	tomatoes, seeded and diced

Sauté the onion and corn in oil about 3 minutes or until softened. Add the squash, sauces, and spices. Continue to cook another 1 to 2 minutes, stirring frequently, just until the squash is tender-crisp. Then add the tomatoes and cook an additional 3 to 4 minutes. Adjust salt and chile powder to taste.

	vegetable oil
8	corn tortillas

Heat about 1½ inches of vegetable oil to about 300 degrees in a medium-size skillet. Immerse the tortillas one at a time to soften and seal. Remove from oil and lay flat on paper towels.

ASSEMBLY AND PRESENTATION

1	pound Monterey jack or Cheddar cheese, shredded

Place grated cheese on a tortilla and then top with a second and fold over. Place quesadillas on a cookie sheet and bake immediately at 350 degrees, just long enough to melt the cheese.

½	head iceberg lettuce, thinly sliced
4	ounces crumbled queso fresco or grated Parmesan cheese

Place the quesadillas on sliced lettuce and spoon vegetables over the top. Garnish with cheese.

STORAGE, FREEZING, AND ADVANCE PREPARATION

The vegetable combination may be made ahead and reheated; however, take care to undercook slightly.

MARIANITOS

This is a simple recipe that was unique at Mariano's because of his freshly made corn tortillas. I have included it because of its popularity, simplicity, and overall appeal.

1–2 *tablespoons refried beans*
1   *ounce Cheddar cheese, grated*
1   *ounce Monterey jack cheese, grated*
1–2 *avocado slices*
     fresh lime juice

Have ready the beans, cheeses, and avocado. Sprinkle lime juice over the avocado to retard browning.

     safflower oil
1   *corn tortilla*

In a small skillet, heat 1½ inches of oil to 350 degrees. Dip each tortilla briefly to soften and seal, pat dry, and then spread with beans and cheeses and fold.

ASSEMBLY AND PRESENTATION

     romaine or *Boston lettuce leaves*
     picante sauce or *Pico de Gallo*
     (see p. 40)

Sauté on a medium-hot griddle about 30 seconds on each side, just long enough to melt the cheese.

Garnish each Marianito with an avocado slice and serve atop a lettuce leaf.

Serve with your favorite salsa or Pico de Gallo.

STORAGE, FREEZING, AND ADVANCE PREPARATION

The ingredients may be prepared ahead; however, Marianitos are best when made to order.

ONION AND CHEESE QUESADILLAS

This is one of those simple but delicious combinations. If you can, either make or obtain fresh flour tortillas—the dish will taste even better. The recipe is quite mild; therefore, this is a good use for your favorite salsa or relish.

1   *onion, thinly sliced*
2   *tablespoons unsalted butter*

In a medium-size skillet, sauté the onion in butter until soft and translucent. Do not brown.

6   *flour tortillas, preferably fresh*

On a hot, seasoned comal or in a microwave oven, briefly warm the tortillas and wrap in a hot towel to keep warm.

ASSEMBLY AND PRESENTATION

½   *cup sour cream*
4–6 *ounces Monterey jack cheese, grated*
6   *cilantro sprigs*

While the onions are still warm, spoon into the tortillas along with sour cream, cheese, and cilantro. Fold over and heat again on a comal or in a microwave oven very briefly, just long enough to melt the cheese.

thinly sliced lettuce
chopped tomatoes
Tila's Red Sauce (see p. 37) or
Green Chile Salsa (see p. 39)

Garnish with lettuce and tomato, and serve with your favorite salsa or relish.

VARIATION

The possibilities are limited only by your imagination. However, one or a combination of the following is delicious: sautéed bulk chorizo, sliced chiles, either mild green chiles or jalapeño chiles or poblano chiles, and slices of avocado.

CHIMICHANGAS

This Arizona specialty is finding its way into Texas restaurants. La Hacienda uses its own Green Chile Salsa with fresh cilantro, or use your favorite recipe or try another recipe from the salsa section.

½   *green bell pepper, chopped*
½   *onion, chopped*
1–2 *tablespoons vegetable oil*

In a medium-size skillet, sauté pepper and onion in hot oil until soft and translucent.

1   *cup shredded cooked chicken* or *chicken filling (see p. 46)*
½   *cup Tila's Red Sauce (see p. 37)* or *Pico de Gallo (see p. 40)* *chicken stock, if needed*

Stir in chicken, sauce, and stock, if needed, to make a soft, moist filling. Set aside.

2   *12-inch, burrito-size flour tortillas*

Using a hot comal, briefly warm the tortillas on one side to soften. You may also do this in a microwave oven for 10 seconds, on high. Cover the second tortilla with a damp cloth while filling the first.

ASSEMBLY AND PRESENTATION

peanut oil for frying

Fill each softened tortilla with half the chicken mixture. Roll the tortilla, folding the edges in, like an egg roll. Secure with 2 toothpicks. Deep-fry in hot oil until slightly brown and crisp. Drain on paper towels.

½   *cup Green Chile Salsa (see p. 39)*
3   *tablespoons Cheddar cheese, shredded*
3   *tablespoons Monterey jack cheese, shredded*

Cover the fried tortillas with Green Chile Salsa and the two cheeses. Place under the broiler just long enough to melt the cheese.

Guacamole (see p. 112)
sour cream
cherry tomatoes

Garnish with Guacamole, sour cream, and cherry tomatoes and serve.

GORDITAS

Gorditas are fat little tortillas made from fresh corn masa, then fried and split to hold various fillings. Cappy makes the masa into little cups, a more attractive and practical approach.

THE FILLING

3–4 cups picadillo (see p. 172)
1½ cups Guacamole (see p. 112)
1 head lettuce, shredded
3 tomatoes, diced
12 ounces Cheddar cheese, grated

Have the picadillo and the Guacamole ready. Have the lettuce shredded, the tomatoes diced, and the cheese grated. Refrigerate.

THE MASA CUPS

fresh corn masa (1–2 ounces per mold)
peanut oil for frying

Spray 3-inch tin molds with a nonstick vegetable coating. Press masa into each mold, and, using tongs, deep-fry in hot oil at 375 degrees. The molds will sink to the bottom and the masa will soon separate from the molds. Turn to lightly brown on both sides, about 2 minutes. Take care not to overcook or the shells will be tough.

ASSEMBLY AND PRESENTATION

sour cream

Place about ¼ to ⅓ cup picadillo in each masa cup. Top with 1 ounce of Cheddar cheese in each shell. Top this with shredded lettuce, Guacamole, diced tomatoes, and sour cream. Serve immediately.

AUTHOR'S NOTE

If fresh masa is not available, use masa harina, prepared according to the package directions. Tin molds can be found in most specialty shops.

STORAGE, FREEZING, AND ADVANCE PREPARATION

The picadillo may be prepared several days ahead. The lettuce, tomatoes, and cheese may be prepared 3 hours ahead. However, for best results, fry the masa cups just prior to serving.

CHICKEN CHILAQUILES

Chilaquiles must have originated in an effort to use stale corn tortillas; however, this delicious dish is well worth creating, even if you have to buy fresh tortillas and toast them. Use a buttered 9-by-12-inch casserole dish or a standard loaf pan. When preparing the ingredients, keep in mind that the amounts are flexible.

2 *onions, chopped* 1 *clove garlic, minced* 2–3 *tablespoons bacon fat*	In a medium-size skillet, sauté the onions and garlic in bacon fat until soft and translucent, about 5 to 8 minutes.
2 *1-pound cans tomatoes, coarsely chopped, including juice* 1 *13-ounce can Rotel tomatoes and chiles* 1 *teaspoon salt* or *to taste* ½ *teaspoon black pepper* ½–1 *teaspoon chile powder*	Stir the tomatoes and their juice into the onions. Season to taste with salt, pepper, and chile powder.
1 *dozen tortillas*	Cut the tortillas in half and then toast in a preheated 350-degree oven for about 8 minutes.

ASSEMBLY AND PRESENTATION

2 *cups cooked chicken, cut in bite-size pieces* 10–12 *ounces Monterey jack cheese, grated* 1–1½ *cups sour cream*	Making 2 or 3 layers and ending with the cheese on top, layer the tortillas, sauce, chicken, and cheese. Bake in a preheated 350-degree oven for about 30 minutes. During the last 5 minutes of cooking time, spread with a moderately thick layer of sour cream. If using a loaf pan, increase the cooking time by about 8 minutes.
minced fresh parsley or *cilantro*	Garnish with parsley or cilantro when serving. Accompany with a fresh steamed vegetable or a fruit salad.

STORAGE, FREEZING, AND
ADVANCE PREPARATION

You may prepare this casserole 12 hours in advance or the day before, refrigerating overnight. It will freeze quite well; thaw completely before baking.

SOFT CHICKEN TACOS

This light and low-calorie sauce is my favorite at La Fogata; it is also served over huevos rancheros. These chicken tacos are a unique item at La Fogata.

½	onion, cut in thin strips	In a large skillet, sauté the onion and pepper in 2 tablespoons hot oil until the onions are soft and translucent, 5 to 8 minutes.
1	bell pepper, cut in thin strips	
2	tablespoons vegetable oil	

2   tablespoons vegetable oil
½   the tomatoes from a 14½–16-ounce can Italian-style tomatoes, including all the juice

Roughly chop the tomatoes and stir into the onion-and-pepper mixture.

1   4-ounce can tomato sauce
2   tablespoons pimiento, diced
¼   teaspoon garlic powder
½   teaspoon salt
¼   teaspoon pepper
3¼   cups chicken stock

Add tomato sauce, pimiento, seasonings, and chicken stock, and cook about 7 minutes. Reduce heat and simmer 20 to 30 minutes. The sauce may cook slowly for an additional 30 to 45 minutes, thus reducing and thickening without adding flour, or add flour as follows.

1½   tablespoons flour (optional)

In a small measure, stir 1½ tablespoons flour into about 1 cup of the sauce to make a smooth paste. Then add this mixture to the sauce and cook an additional 5 to 10 minutes, or until the flour is cooked and the sauce thickened. Adjust seasonings.

3   chicken breasts (singles)

Simmer the chicken, in enough water to cover, about 20 minutes or until cooked but still tender. Remove skin and bones and then shred the meat in small pieces.

    vegetable oil
10   corn tortillas

In a medium-size skillet, heat oil to about 300 degrees. Pass tortillas into hot oil for a few seconds to soften and seal. Remove carefully and set aside between paper towels. Do this just prior to assembly.

ASSEMBLY AND
PRESENTATION

Dip the tortillas in the sauce and then fill with the shredded chicken, moistened with a small amount of the sauce. Roll up and place seam side down in a casserole dish. Bake, covered, to heat, about 10 to 12 minutes. Top with additional sauce when serving.

STORAGE, FREEZING, AND
ADVANCE PREPARATION

The sauce may be made several days in advance; however, these soft tacos are best when made with freshly cooked and shredded chicken. While you may make them ahead and then reheat, you will lose some of the quality that makes this dish so special.

TURNOVERS ENVUELTOS

This rich tomato sauce is flavored with cheese. You will find many other uses for it. Like a Welsh rarebit, it can turn a toasted cheese or cheese-and-chile sandwich into a special and satisfying meal. Also good on omelets or meatloaf.

2 *cloves garlic, minced* ¼ *cup bacon fat, vegetable oil,* or 　*rendered beef* or *pork fat* 5 *tablespoons flour* 1½ *cups tomato sauce* 1–2 *teaspoons ground cumin* ⅛–¼ *teaspoon red pepper* 3–4 *cups hot water* or *beef stock*	Sauté garlic until soft in bacon fat or vegetable oil or rendered fat. Rendered fat will have a richer taste than vegetable oil. Stir in flour and cook until nut brown in color. This is your roux. In a blender or a food processor fitted with a metal blade, process this cooked roux 2 to 3 seconds. With the machine on, pour in the tomato sauce, seasonings, and 1 cup hot water or stock. Process until smooth. Use the greater amount of red pepper for a moderately spicy sauce.
3–4 *ounces Cheddar* or *Monterey jack cheese, finely grated*	Transfer the entire mixture to a 1½-quart saucepan and cook over medium heat, adding the cheese in 4 to 5 batches. Add the remaining water or stock, then stir 5 to 8 minutes or until smooth. Set aside.
1 *onion, diced* 1–2 *tablespoons vegetable oil*	In a large skillet, sauté the onion in the vegetable oil until soft and translucent.
2 *pounds ground beef* or *4 cups shredded cooked chicken* *salt and pepper to taste*	If using beef, stir in and cook 5 to 8 minutes, or until juices no longer run pink. If using chicken, stir it in and cook just long enough to heat. Add ½ cup of the prepared sauce. Season to taste.

	vegetable oil	In a medium-size skillet, heat oil to about 300 degrees. Pass tortillas into hot oil for a few seconds to soften and seal. Remove carefully and set aside between paper towels. Do this just prior to assembly.
8	*corn tortillas*	

ASSEMBLY AND PRESENTATION

chopped tomatoes or *Pico de Gallo (see p. 40)* or *Mexican Cream (see p. 45)*

Fill each tortilla with beef or chicken and fold over, making a half-moon shape. Cover with foil to keep warm.

Nap with heated sauce and, if desired, garnish with chopped tomatoes, Pico de Gallo, or Mexican Cream.

STORAGE, FREEZING, AND ADVANCE PREPARATION

The sauce may be made several days ahead. When reheating, whisk vigorously to restore texture. Envueltos are best when assembled just prior to serving.

GREEN CHICKEN ENCHILADAS

Green enchiladas are almost a staple in parts of Texas, but the secret in this recipe is Carmen Calvillo's green sauce. Customers always request her recipe—it's the cilantro that makes it distinct.

1¼	pound tomatilloes, quartered
½	cup water
1	clove garlic, whole
2	serrano chiles
¼	teaspoon salt
¼	teaspoon pepper
⅓	cup cilantro leaves, loosely packed, chopped
	chicken stock, if needed

Boil the tomatilloes in ½ cup water with garlic, chiles, and salt and pepper until soft, about 15 to 20 minutes.

Puree the cooked sauce in a blender to liquefy. While blending, add washed cilantro leaves. Set aside. The sauce yield is about 2½ cups. It will thicken upon standing, and you may need to thin with chicken stock.

2	whole chicken breasts
	salt
1	cup chicken stock

Simmer the chicken in lightly salted water until tender, about 10 to 15 minutes. Cool chicken will be slightly undercooked. Shred the cooked chicken and then, just prior to serving, heat in 1 cup chicken stock. This will heat the chicken without overcooking.

1	cup peanut oil
8	corn tortillas

In a medium-size skillet, heat oil to about 300 degrees. Pass tortillas into hot oil for a few seconds to soften and seal. Remove carefully and set aside between paper towels. Do this just prior to assembly.

ASSEMBLY AND PRESENTATION

1   cup sour cream
1   pound   Mozzarella   cheese,
     grated

Fill softened tortillas with shredded chicken and 1–2 tablespoons of the sauce. Roll up and place seam side down in a casserole. Pour the green sauce over the top, and garnish with sour cream and cheese. Place in a hot oven 5 to 8 minutes or just long enough to melt the cheese.

Serve with Guacamole Salad (see p. 112) or fresh fruit.

STORAGE, FREEZING, AND ADVANCE PREPARATION

The sauce may be made a day in advance; however, the dish is best when the chicken is freshly prepared.

NINFA'S GREEN ENCHILADAS

Ninfa's version of green enchiladas is quite different from those at La Fogata or other restaurants. Her use of green tomatoes with tomatilloes gives a distinctive and delicious taste.

3½–4 cups Chicken Stew (see p. 46)

Prepare the filling according to the directions and then set aside.

10–12 tomatilloes, quartered
3   green tomatoes, quartered
2   cloves garlic
1–2   jalapeño chiles, stemmed, seeded,
         and chopped
6   cilantro sprigs
½   teaspoon salt or to taste
2   tablespoons vegetable oil
         pinch of sugar
         chicken stock, if needed

In a medium-size skillet, sauté the tomatilloes, tomatoes, garlic, and jalapeños in just enough water to prevent sticking, for about 8 to 10 minutes or until soft. Transfer to a blender jar along with the cilantro and blend until smooth, in 2 batches. Adjust salt to taste, then return mixture to the same skillet with vegetable oil and simmer 2 to 3 minutes. Add sugar and adjust seasoning. It may be necessary to add some chicken stock to achieve a sauce that is thin enough to pour over the enchiladas.

½–1 cup vegetable oil
12   corn tortillas, preferably thin

Heat the oil in a small skillet, using enough to immerse each tortilla briefly to soften and seal. Press between paper towels to remove excess moisture.

ASSEMBLY AND PRESENTATION

12   ounces Monterey jack cheese,
         grated

When all the tortillas are softened, divide the filling between them, using about ¼ cup for each one. Dip each tortilla in the sauce, then roll to enclose the filling, and place seam side down in individual dishes or an oblong baking dish. Sprinkle with the grated cheese. Place in a preheated 350-degree oven for about 10 minutes to warm thoroughly.

1½   *cups sour cream*

STORAGE, FREEZING, AND ADVANCE PREPARATION

Serve napped with additional sauce and garnish with sour cream.

Both the sauce and the filling may be made up to 2 days in advance. You may fill the tortillas 12 hours in advance and then refrigerate until ready to heat. Bring them to room temperature and then bake, covered, for 10 to 15 minutes. Remember, if you do not allow them to warm up at room temperature, be sure to allow for additional cooking time.

POBLANO AND CHEESE ENCHILADAS

The roasted and peeled poblano chiles make these enchiladas extraordinary. You may use Muenster cheese, or Clive Duval suggests combining two or all of the suggested cheeses according to your personal taste. This dish is quite rich and needs only an interesting wine and perhaps a steamed vegetable.

½   cup milk
½   cup sour cream
1   tablespoon fresh lime juice
     salt and black pepper to taste

Whisk the cream sauce ingredients together by hand. Set aside at room temperature for several hours. Refrigerate if not using immediately.

2½–3 cups Tila's Red Sauce (see p. 37)

Prepare the salsa, then set aside.

6   poblano chiles, roasted and peeled
2   medium-size white onions, halved and cut in narrow strips
½   stick butter
½   cup, more or less, heavy cream
½   cup, more or less, sour cream
     salt and pepper to taste

Cut the chiles into strips about ¼ by 2½ inches. In a medium-size skillet, sauté the onions in butter 15 minutes or until softened. Add the chile strips, then stir in creams and simmer 3 to 4 minutes. Taste, adding salt and pepper as desired. Set aside while preparing the tortillas.

ASSEMBLY AND PRESENTATION

½–1 cup vegetable oil
12   corn tortillas
8–10 ounces Muenster, Jarlsberg, baby Swiss, or Havarti cheese, grated

In a medium-size skillet, heat the oil to about 300 degrees. Dip each tortilla in the hot oil to soften and seal and then press between paper towels to drain.

Dip each tortilla in the prepared salsa, and then fill with the pepper mixture and 2–3 tablespoons grated cheese. Roll up and place seam side down in individual baking dishes. Pour the remaining sauce over the top. Place in a hot 375-degree oven just long enough to heat through and melt the cheese, about 10 to 15 minutes. Add more grated cheese during the final 5 minutes of baking time.

shredded lettuce
chopped tomatoes
reserved cream sauce

When ready to serve, top with lettuce and tomatoes and spoon some of the cream sauce over the top.

VARIATION

Add 10 ounces chopped fresh spinach to the pepper mixture during the final 2 to 3 minutes of cooking time.

STORAGE, FREEZING, AND ADVANCE PREPARATION

The salsa, the pepper mixture, and the cream sauce may all be prepared early in the day or a day in advance. Assembly and baking are best done just prior to serving or not more than 2 hours ahead.

NINFA'S CRAB ENCHILADAS

This is Ninfa's special version—a delightfully delicate dish when made with thin corn tortillas. I have taken the liberty of soaking the enchiladas in cream, which makes an even lighter dish, almost reminiscent of crepes.

1 *medium-size white onion, chopped*	In a medium-size skillet, sauté the onion, tomatoes, and chile in butter for about 8 minutes. Add seasonings and then remove and set aside.
3 *large tomatoes, peeled and chopped*	
1 *jalapeño chile, stemmed, seeded, and minced*	
½ *stick butter*	
½ *teaspoon salt* or *to taste*	
¼ *teaspoon white pepper*	

1 *pound fresh or thawed frozen crabmeat*	In the same skillet, sauté the crabmeat in butter several minutes or just long enough to heat through. Stir in half the reserved sauce and set aside.
3–4 *tablespoons butter*	

½–¾ *cup safflower oil* or *clarified butter*	In a medium-size skillet, heat the oil or butter to about 300 degrees. Dip each tortilla in the oil or butter briefly to soften and seal, about 10 seconds, then press between paper towels to drain.
12 *thin corn tortillas*	

ASSEMBLY AND PRESENTATION

1 *cup light cream*	Divide the filling between the tortillas, then fold and place seam side down in a buttered 8½-by-11-inch baking dish. Pour the cream over the tortillas and then cover and let soak for 1 hour at room temperature or 3 to 4 hours refrigerated.

2 *cups (about 8 ounces) Monterey jack cheese, grated*	Spoon the remaining sauce over the soaked enchiladas, then top with grated cheese and bake in a preheated 375-degree oven for about 10 to 15 minutes or until heated through.

fresh cilantro or *watercress*

Garnish with fresh cilantro or watercress.

Serve with wedges of seasonal fruits, such as melon or papaya, or a spinach-stuffed tomato, or a spinach soufflé.

STORAGE, FREEZING, AND ADVANCE PREPARATION

You may make the enchiladas early in the day, allowing them to soak in the cream. Prepare the sauce also, refrigerating until ready to bake. These enchiladas also may be frozen, providing the crab is fresh. Return to room temperature before baking and increase the baking time to 25 minutes.

SAN MIGUEL'S CRABMEAT ENCHILADAS

1   *cup sour cream*
½   *cup milk* or *half-and-half*
    pinch of salt

Mix together the sour cream and milk or half-and-half. Add a pinch of salt to taste. Set aside.

1   *pound sea scallops*
3   *tablespoons butter*
1   *tablespoon vegetable oil*
1   *pound lump crabmeat*
1   *clove garlic, minced*

If the scallops are large, cut into small pieces. In a medium-size skillet, melt the butter and vegetable oil. Stir in the crabmeat, scallops, garlic, and half the cream mixture, reserving the remaining half for the topping. Cook about 3 to 5 minutes, stirring constantly over medium heat, just until the scallops are firm.

    vegetable oil
10 *corn tortillas, preferably thin*

In another skillet, heat 1½ inches of oil to about 300 degrees. Pass the tortillas into hot oil for a few seconds to soften and seal. Remove carefully and set aside between paper towels. Do this just prior to assembly.

ASSEMBLY AND PRESENTATION

1½–2 *cups Monterey jack cheese, grated*

Roll the crabmeat mixture into the tortillas and place side by side in a baking dish. Top with grated cheese, then the reserved sour cream mixture, and cover loosely with foil. Bake in a 350-degree oven for 20 minutes, then uncover and bake another 5 minutes.

VARIATION

I have soaked these enchiladas in 1 cup heavy cream for 2 hours before baking and found the results excellent. Try serving them on fresh, lightly steamed spinach leaves or fresh Texas watercress for a creative touch.

FONDA SAN MIGUEL

STORAGE, FREEZING, AND
ADVANCE PREPARATION

If using fresh crabmeat, the enchiladas may be filled, rolled, and frozen. Brush them with warm, heavy cream before freezing. Add the cheese and sour cream mixture after the enchiladas have thawed, prior to baking.

SHRIMP ENCHILADAS

1 medium-size onion, chopped
2 bell peppers, chopped
1 tablespoon butter
1 1-pound can tomatoes, chopped, including juice
2 cups tomato sauce
1/4 teaspoon garlic salt
1/2 teaspoon leaf oregano
1/4 teaspoon white pepper
1/2–1 cup water or clam juice

In a large skillet or sauté pan, sauté the onion and peppers in butter until soft and translucent, about 5 to 8 minutes.

Add the tomatoes and tomato sauce, spices, and water or clam juice, and simmer 20 to 30 minutes.

1/2 stick butter
2 tablespoons flour
1/2 cup hot water

Using a blender or a food processor fitted with a metal blade, blend the butter and flour with 1/2 cup hot water and 1 cup of the sauce until smooth. Whisk this puree into the remaining sauce and cook an additional 10 minutes, stirring occasionally. Add more water or clam juice if necessary to thin the sauce.

1 1/2–2 pounds cooked shrimp, coarsely chopped

Mix the shrimp with about 1 cup of the sauce or enough to moisten, and set aside.

vegetable oil
12 corn tortillas

Just prior to assembly, use a medium-size skillet and heat at least 1 1/2 inches of oil to about 300 degrees. Pass the tortillas into hot oil for a few seconds to soften and seal. Remove carefully and set aside between paper towels.

ASSEMBLY AND PRESENTATION

minced fresh parsley

Dip each tortilla into the sauce and then fill them with the shrimp. Roll to enclose filling. Place seam side down in a casserole or au gratin dish.

Pour the sauce over the top, using just enough to give a good coating. Then bake covered at 350 degrees, just long enough to reheat, about 10 to 15 minutes.

Serve with the remaining sauce on the side and garnish with minced parsley.

VARIATION

Combine the shrimp with 6 ounces crumbled *queso fresco* or California goat cheese, or use one of these cheeses for a garnish. Crumble atop the warm enchiladas and return to the oven about 2 to 3 minutes to reheat.

STORAGE, FREEZING, AND ADVANCE PREPARATION

The sauce may be prepared in advance and either refrigerated or frozen; however, for best results, cook the shrimp fresh and assemble just prior to serving.

FROM CLIVE DUVAL

When preparing enchiladas, first dip the tortillas in oil to soften and seal. Press between paper towels to remove the excess oil and then dip into the sauce before filling and rolling.

AUTHOR'S CONTRIBUTION

When preparing enchiladas in advance, pour some cream over them before refrigerating or freezing. Allow 30 minutes and then freeze or refrigerate until ready to reheat. The cream softens the tortillas; however, if they are first sealed in oil, they will not fall apart.

Main Dishes

TILA'S
Spit-roasted Chickens with Avocado and Lettuce Salad
Grilled Swordfish with Fried Potatoes

Avocados and Pico de Gallo
Grilled Skirt Steaks
Avocado, Lettuce, and Tomato Salad

MAIN DISHES

Plato Emilio	Cafe Cancún
Roast Suckling Pig with Fruit Garnishes	Las Canarias
Paella Levantina	Las Canarias
Acapulco K-Bobs	Ernesto's
Pollo Pibil	Fonda San Miguel
Grilled Peppers with Chicken	La Fogata
Meatballs	Los Panchos
Chiles with Nut Sauce	Los Panchos
Avocado Zapata	Los Tres Bobos
Shrimp in Salsa Diabla	Mario's and Alberto's
Cappy's Scallops with Chile Cream Sauce	Cappy's
Shrimp and Crabmeat Crepes Veracruzanas	Ernesto's
Flounder Veracruzana	The Tavern
Fish in Garlic Sauce	Fonda San Miguel
Marinero Fish	Mario's and Alberto's
Stuffed Snapper	Ernesto's
Mario's Shrimp in Garlic Sauce	Mario's and Alberto's
Grilling Marinade for Flank Steaks and Skirt Steaks	Tila's
Marinade for Spit-Roasted Chickens	Tila's
Ninfa's Marinade	Ninfa's
Grilled Shrimp	Author's Contribution
Grilled Swordfish	Tila's

PLATO EMILIO

This may seem an extravagant use of beef tenderloin; however, it is traditional among the best Mexican American cooks to choose this tender cut for many beef dishes. This is a very popular dish at Cafe Cancún.

3 medium-size red potatoes	Drop the potatoes in lightly salted boiling water and boil 5 minutes. Peel and cut in ½-inch cubes.
4 tablespoons vegetable oil 1–1½ pounds beef tenderloin, cut in cubes 1 large green pepper, seeded and chopped 1 large yellow onion, chopped 2 large tomatoes, peeled and coarsely chopped tomato juice or beef stock, if needed salt and pepper to taste	In a large skillet, heat the oil and sauté the potatoes until browned on all sides. Remove and set aside. In the same skillet, over medium-high heat, add the beef, pepper, and onion, using more oil if necessary. Cook to brown the beef, 4 to 5 minutes. Return potatoes to the skillet, add the tomatoes, and simmer, covered, until the meat is tender, about 8 to 10 minutes. Check often, as it may be necessary to add tomato juice or beef stock if too much of the liquid evaporates. The juices and tomato will reduce, making a thick and rich-tasting sauce. Season to taste with salt and pepper.

PRESENTATION

avocado slices

Serve the stew with your favorite rice or with homemade flour tortillas. Garnish with avocado slices.

STORAGE, FREEZING, AND ADVANCE PREPARATION

The stew may be made a day in advance and reheated. It freezes successfully for 3 to 4 months.

ROAST SUCKLING PIG
WITH FRUIT GARNISHES

This is a colorful dish for a special occasion. It is time-consuming but guaranteed to wow your guests.

1	11–13-pound suckling pig, thawed and cleaned

At least 2 days in advance, begin the marinade.

THE MARINADE

3	cloves garlic
2	teaspoons salt
½	teaspoon black pepper
⅓	cup soy sauce
3	cups red wine
1	cup olive oil or vegetable oil
¼	cup vinegar
2	yellow onions, thinly sliced

Combine the marinade ingredients in a plastic bag large enough to accommodate the pig. Marinate the pig, refrigerated, for 1 to 2 days. Turn several times to insure even basting.

THE PIG

1	teaspoon ground ginger
1	teaspoon dry mustard
1	teaspoon rosemary leaves
1	teaspoon salt
½	teaspoon ground cloves
½	teaspoon sage
½	teaspoon pepper
3	tablespoons olive oil
8–10	cloves garlic, crushed

Remove the pig, strain the marinade, and reserve 2 cups. Combine the seasonings and olive oil and rub onto pig. Make 8 to 10 slashes and insert a crushed clove of garlic in each. Wrap the pig's feet, nose, ears, and tail with foil to prevent burning. Use a large roasting pan that will accommodate the pig when fitted on a rack.

4	carrots, thickly sliced
1	onion, sliced
3	cups apple juice
2	cups strained marinade

Place carrots and onion beneath the pig. Using poultry skewers, pin the ears back and tuck front feet under and back feet forward, securing with string if necessary. Combine the apple juice and reserved marinade and pour into roasting pan. Place in a preheated 450-degree oven.

After 15 minutes, reduce heat to 300 degrees and bake, covered with foil, for 2½ hours. Then uncover and continue baking an additional hour to insure crisp skin. Increase the oven temperature if necessary.

THE FRIED BANANAS

¾   *cup biscuit mix*
½   *cup shredded coconut*
4   *bananas, halved lengthwise, then quartered*
2   *eggs*
1   *tablespoon water*
1   *teaspoon oil*
     oil for frying

Combine biscuit mix with coconut and set aside. Peel and cut bananas in 4 quarters. Beat eggs with 1 tablespoon water and 1 teaspoon oil. Dip each banana in egg and then roll in coconut-biscuit mixture, pressing to be sure coating adheres.

Heat the oil to 375 degrees and deep-fry bananas until crisp and golden. Drain on paper towels and set aside. Serve as soon as possible after frying.

ASSEMBLY AND PRESENTATION

8   *fresh pineapple slices*
8   *fresh orange slices*
8   *fresh strawberries*

     Black Beans (see p. 125)
     cooked white rice
     chopped tomatoes
     chopped scallions
     Mexican Cream (see p. 45)

Arrange a slice of pineapple with an orange slice and then secure a strawberry with a toothpick. Repeat until you have 8 fruit garnishes.

Present the pig on a large platter with the fruit garnishes. Accompany with beans and rice. Offer additional garnish bowls of chopped tomatoes, scallions, and Mexican Cream.

AUTHOR'S NOTE

Leftover pork is delicious sliced and served cold with mango chutney or jalapeño jelly.

STORAGE, FREEZING, AND ADVANCE PREPARATION

Many of the accompaniments may be made in advance, particularly the beans and the rice. Garnishes may be prepared early on the day you plan to serve the pig. However, the bananas are best when fried just prior to serving.

PAELLA LEVANTINA

The very nature of paella makes the recipe somewhat inexact with regard to the liquid needed to finish the dish. Use your own judgment, adding enough to keep the rice from drying out, taking care not to overcook.

THE SIFRITO

1	pound pork tenderloin, cut in ¼-inch cubes
2–3	tablespoons olive oil
1	large onion, sliced
2	green peppers, thinly sliced
2	cloves garlic, minced
½	teaspoon salt
¼	teaspoon pepper
1	tomato, diced

In a large skillet, sauté pork in olive oil, adding onion and green peppers as the pork browns. Cook 3 minutes and add seasonings and tomatoes. Remove from heat. This makes about 2½ cups.

THE PAELLA LEVANTINA

8	chicken pieces, preferably thighs or breasts
2–3	tablespoons vegetable oil
6	cups chicken stock
3–4	threads saffron
3	cups long-grain rice, cooked
3	lobster tails, meat removed
12	slices smoked Spanish sausage
12	clams, in shells
12	medium-size shrimp, peeled and deveined (leave tails intact)

In a large skillet, sauté the chicken in oil on both sides until brown, about 12 minutes. Set aside. The chicken will not be fully cooked.

Boil stock and saffron together for 2 minutes and let steep 5 to 10 minutes.

Place the sifrito, stock, rice, lobster, and sausage in a large baking dish or paella pan and bring to a boil. Arrange the chicken, clams, and shrimp on top of the other ingredients, and then bake, covered, in a preheated 375-degree oven for 20 minutes. You may need to adjust the amount of liquid as the paella bakes, adding more during the baking time or straining off excess if some remains after cooking.

PRESENTATION

1 package frozen green peas, cooked
8–10 artichoke hearts, halved (optional)

Garnish the paella with cooked peas and/or artichoke hearts, if desired.

AUTHOR'S NOTE

Cook the rice according to the package instructions, but reduce the cooking time by 8 minutes, so the rice is slightly undercooked. Sautéing the rice in a small amount of oil before adding the liquid will help prevent it from sticking together.

STORAGE, FREEZING, AND ADVANCE PREPARATION

The paella may be frozen after the sifrito, rice, chicken, and sausage have been combined and partially cooked. Add the shellfish after thawing, during reheating. During the first baking, before freezing, reduce the time from 20 minutes to about 12. Paella is an excellent party dish and is easily prepared several days ahead, using several steps. This result will be better than freezing the paella. *The Day Before*: Prepare the sifrito. Cook the rice. Sauté the chicken, cooking slightly longer than the recipe suggests. *The Day of Your Party*: Assemble the dish for baking. Be sure the refrigerated ingredients return to room temperature before baking.

ACAPULCO K-BOBS

Ernesto developed this unusual combination of beef, chicken, and shrimp, a typical Mexican American grilled specialty. The unique butter sauce is his trademark.

THE SAUCE

2	*green onions, thinly sliced*
2	*sticks unsalted butter, cut in 10 pieces*
½	*tablespoon vinegar*
1–2	*ounces orange liqueur*
1	*fresh pineapple slice, diced*
½	*tablespoon soy sauce*
2	*tablespoons shredded coconut, preferably fresh*

In a large skillet over medium-low heat, simmer the green onions in 1 tablespoon butter, vinegar, and liqueur until soft. Add pineapple and then whisk in more butter, 1 piece at a time, over low heat. Do not allow the butter to simmer or it will separate. Whisk constantly to achieve a creamy consistency, lifting the pan from the heat if necessary to control the temperature. Stir in the soy sauce and coconut. The sauce may be held in a double boiler over hot water; however, do not place over heat.

2	*seedless oranges*
	fresh lime juice
	vegetable oil

Peel and halve oranges, cutting a thin slice from the base of each so they will remain flat. Grill the oranges on a roasting pan 4 inches from the broiling element. Brush with lime juice and oil and grill until hot and lightly browned. Keep warm.

THE K-BOBS

½	*pound beef tenderloin, cut in 1-inch cubes*
2	*boneless chicken breasts (singles), cut in 1-inch cubes*
6	*jumbo shrimp, peeled, deveined, and butterflied (leave tails intact)*

For the k-bobs, use an outdoor grill with medium-hot heat or an indoor grill on highest heat. If necessary, k-bobs may be oven-broiled 4 inches from the broiling element; watch them closely so they do not burn.

THE BASTING LIQUID

⅓	*cup peanut oil*
2	*tablespoons soy sauce*
	juice of 3–4 limes

In a small saucer, stir together the peanut oil and soy sauce for basting. Squeeze the lime juice into a separate saucer.

ASSEMBLY AND PRESENTATION

8	*medium-size crisp white mushrooms*
½	*fresh pineapple, peeled and cut in 1-inch cubes*

Alternate the beef, chicken, and shrimp with mushrooms and pineapple chunks on skewers. Brush liberally with lime juice and then with oil and soy sauce. Grill, turning to brown all sides, basting several times. Depending on the cooking source, time varies from 2 to 5 minutes per side. Transfer to serving plates and remove skewers.

2	*cups cooked white rice prepared oranges minced fresh parsley*

Serve the k-bobs atop the rice, lightly napped with sauce. Nap the oranges with sauce and then sprinkle with minced parsley.

STORAGE, FREEZING, AND ADVANCE PREPARATION

The beef, chicken, and shrimp may be put on skewers earlier in the day. The sauce may be prepared 3 hours before serving and held over hot water (100 degrees or less) or in a thermos bottle.

POLLO PIBIL

San Miguel serves an interpretation of Diana Kennedy's authentic recipes. Chef Mike Ravago takes great pride in his food, and his own special touches make his dishes unique and delicious.

1	tablespoon achiote seeds
¼	cup water
¼	teaspoon cumin seeds
¼	teaspoon leaf oregano
3	whole allspice
4	cloves garlic, minced
1	tablespoon salt
¼	cup fresh orange juice
1	tablespoon red wine vinegar
6	chicken breasts (singles)
	banana leaves

At least one day ahead, cover the achiote seeds with ¼ cup water and bring to a boil. Soak overnight.

With a mortar and pestle or spice grinder, grind the seasonings together and then grind in the seeds with their liquid, orange juice, and vinegar.

Trim excess fat from the chicken and remove the skin. Spread with the achiote paste. Reserve about 1 tablespoon to finish the sauce. If available, wrap in banana leaves.

2	tomatoes, peeled and chopped
1	1-pound can Italian-style tomatoes, including juice
1	large onion, thinly sliced
2	tablespoons vegetable oil

In a medium-size skillet, sauté the tomatoes with onion in hot oil until the onion is soft and translucent, about 8 minutes.

Stir in the reserved achiote paste and pour over the chicken. Cover with foil and bake 50 minutes to 1 hour at 350 degrees.

PRESENTATION

fresh herbs
radish roses

To serve, transfer the chicken in the banana leaves to a platter. Return the sauce to a skillet and bring to a boil. Spoon over the chicken. Garnish with fresh herbs, such as parsley, cilantro, or watercress, and radish roses.

VARIATION

This dish may also be served buffet style. Remove the chicken from the bone and cut into bite-size pieces, then combine with the reheated sauce. Serve with plain white rice and either green salad or fruit salad. Both pair nicely with the assertive seasonings of this dish.

STORAGE, FREEZING, AND ADVANCE PREPARATION

The entire dish may be made ahead and reheated. It also freezes quite well; if serving buffet style, freeze before boning and cutting the meat.

GRILLED PEPPERS WITH CHICKEN

The attractive presentation of this off-the-menu dish is what has earned La Fogata its reputation for "nouvelle cuisine." This is a low-calorie recipe, particularly if served with a light tomato sauce. Be sure to note the oven method at the end of the recipe if you do not have an indoor or outdoor grill.

	juice of 1 lime	Squeeze lime juice over the chicken breast. Season to preference, and then grill over a moderate flame, brushing both sides with oil. When cooked and tender, about 12 to 15 minutes, remove the skin and shred the meat. Set aside. Or, bake in a 350-degree oven, seasoning in the same way, for 15 minutes.
1	*chicken breast (single)*	
	garlic salt and pepper to taste	
	oil	
2	*large poblano chiles*	Do not peel the peppers at this time. Wash them and then, using a sharp knife, make a circular cut to remove the stem in one piece, and set it aside. Remove the seeds and veins.
2	*ounces Monterey jack* or *mild Texas goat cheese, cut in small pieces* *chicken stock*	Stuff the prepared peppers with a combination of chicken and cheese, moistened with a scant amount of chicken stock. If using an open grill (indoor or outdoor), return the stuffed peppers to the grill and cook on both sides until the peel is charred. Take care not to burn. Remove, pulling away the peel, and then replace the top for garnish.

PRESENTATION

sour cream or *salsa*	Serve with sour cream or a light tomato salsa. Or note the creamy cheese sauce in the variation.

LA FOGATA

VARIATION

I like to serve this dish with a sauce of sour cream and cheeses. In a small skillet over medium-low heat, stir together 3½ ounces cream cheese and 2 tablespoons grated Parmesan cheese until melted. Add ½ cup sour cream and continue cooking just long enough to heat through. Spoon over the peppers and, if desired, top with chopped pecans, lightly sautéed in butter.

AUTHOR'S NOTE

If you do not have a grill, roast the poblano peppers (see p. 27) and then stuff with chicken and cheese. Brush lightly with melted butter and then bake in a hot, 400-degree oven for 12 to 15 minutes, or just long enough to heat the chicken and melt the cheese.

STORAGE, FREEZING, AND ADVANCE PREPARATION

The chicken may be baked and the peppers stuffed a day in advance. They taste best hot from the grill, especially when cooked outdoors.

MEATBALLS
ALBONDIGAS

These poached meatballs are Spanish in origin—and, up until this year, I had never seen them outside Arizona or some areas of California. They are often used in soup; however, they are delicious with this spicy sauce. You may serve them with rice or pasta. Please note the substitute for the often difficult to obtain chile chipotles.

THE SAUCE

1	4–6 ounce can chile chipotles or 2 tablespoons chile powder, 1 jalapeño chile, stemmed and seeded, and 2 tablespoons tomato paste
2	tomatoes, quartered
¼	yellow onion
1	clove garlic, peeled

In a blender or a food processor fitted with a metal blade, process the chile chipotles and all their juices to puree. Or follow the same procedure with the chile powder, jalapeño, and tomato paste. Add tomatoes, onion, and garlic, and process to puree. Set aside.

THE POACHING LIQUID

1	14½-ounce can chicken or beef stock
1	cup water

In a medium-size skillet, combine the stock and water.

THE MEATBALLS

1	slice bread, torn in fourths
¼	cup whole milk
1	pound ground beef or a combination of ground beef and veal
½	medium-size onion, finely chopped
1	clove garlic, minced
1	tablespoon fresh parsley, minced
1	teaspoon salt
1	egg

Soak the bread in milk for 5 minutes and then combine the meatball ingredients, being sure the egg is completely incorporated.

Shape into meatballs about the size of a large walnut and then drop in the simmering stock and water. Turn and poach over medium heat for about 10 to 12 minutes. Remove the meatballs with a slotted spoon and set aside.

Using a whisk, stir the chipotle sauce into the poaching liquid and cook, uncovered, for 15 minutes or until thickened and reduced. Return the meatballs to the sauce and cook until heated through.

PRESENTATION

Serve both sauce and meatballs with rice or pasta or with thick flour tortillas.

STORAGE, FREEZING, AND ADVANCE PREPARATION

These may be made a day ahead and reheated or frozen for 6 to 9 months.

CHILES WITH NUT SAUCE
CHILES EN NOGADA

Araceli is locally famous for her version of this classic dish. I have suggested sautéing the pecans for a richer flavor.

THE CREAM SAUCE

½   cup heavy cream
1½   cups sour cream
       salt to taste
1   teaspoon fresh lime juice
1–2 tablespoons milk for thinning

Stir together the heavy cream, sour cream, salt, and lime juice. Let stand 2 to 3 hours at room temperature to thicken. Refrigerate but bring to room temperature when ready to serve. If the sauce is extremely thick, thin with milk.

THE PICADILLO

1   pound ground beef
1   clove garlic, minced
2   small onions, chopped
2   tomatoes, peeled and chopped
¼–⅓ cup dark seedless raisins
¼   teaspoon cinnamon
       salt and pepper to taste

In a medium-size skillet, sauté the beef with garlic and onions until lightly browned. Stir in the tomatoes, raisins, cinnamon, and salt and pepper to taste. Simmer about 10 to 15 minutes and then set aside to cool. Skim off excess fat.

THE CHILES

6   poblano chiles, roasted and peeled

Roast and peel the chiles (see p. 27). Using scissors, snip the seeds from the chiles, keeping the stems intact. Make an incision just long enough to allow filling. Stuff with the cooked and cooled beef mixture. If necessary, secure the opening with a toothpick.

THE EGG BATTER

3   eggs, separated
2–3 tablespoons flour
¼   teaspoon salt
⅛   teaspoon pepper

Beat the egg yolks with the flour until very thick. The amount of flour in the batter varies from cook to cook. Use a lesser amount for a thinner, crispier coating. In a separate bowl, beat the whites with salt and pepper to stiff peaks, then fold whites into yolks.

ASSEMBLY AND
PRESENTATION

peanut oil for frying
½   *cup flour in a sifter*

Heat about 3 inches of peanut oil in a deep saucepan or deep-fryer to 375 to 400 degrees. Lightly dust each chile with flour, then dip into the batter (tongs are useful here) and fry one at a time, spooning additional batter over exposed surfaces if necessary. Turn to seal the batter on both sides. Fry 2 to 2½ minutes, turning once again during the frying. Keep warm while repeating the procedure.

1   *cup chopped pecans*
2   *tablespoons butter*

Sauté pecans in butter for 2 to 3 minutes. Drain on paper towels.

½   *cup pomegranate seeds*

Nap each chile with the cream sauce, and then garnish with both pecans and pomegranate seeds.

VARIATION

Spoon cut portions into freshly heated corn or flour tortillas.

STORAGE, FREEZING, AND
ADVANCE PREPARATION

The chiles may be prepared a day in advance and stuffed. For best results, fry just prior to serving.

AVOCADO ZAPATA

John Thorson, one of the owners of Los Tres Bobos, gives Rubén Reyna, the owner of El Turisto Restaurant in Donna, Texas, the credit for this unusual dish. The recipe makes quite a lot of sauce; however, you will find many uses for this light and delicious tomato sauce. The secret ingredient which gives the meat its distinctive flavor is the crushed peanut brittle.

THE SAUCE

½	onion, chopped
1	clove garlic, finely minced
1	medium-size bell pepper, chopped
1	tablespoon vegetable oil
1	8-ounce can tomato sauce
1	1-pound can stewed tomatoes, including juice
	salt and pepper to taste

In a large skillet, sauté onion, garlic, and bell pepper in oil until soft and translucent. Add tomato sauce and stewed tomatoes, using a blending fork to break up whole tomatoes. Simmer 30 minutes over low heat and season to taste with salt and pepper. Set aside until ready to serve.

THE MEAT MIXTURE

1	pound ground beef
½	cup onion, chopped
½	cup raisins
⅓	cup mixed nuts (pecans, almonds, and walnuts), finely chopped, and 1 tablespoon brown sugar or ⅓ cup peanut brittle, crushed
	salt and white pepper to taste
¼–½	cup beef stock

In a large skillet, brown the ground meat with the onion until the meat is fully cooked. Stir in the raisins and the mixed nuts and sugar or the peanut brittle, adding salt and pepper to taste. It may be necessary to stir in some stock if the mixture becomes dry. Set aside.

THE AVOCADOS

4	avocados, peeled and pitted
1	egg

Enlarge the cavity of each avocado half by scooping a small amount of the avocado meat from each one. Chop and stir the removed portion into the egg and then combine with the meat mixture.

THE EGG BATTER

2	eggs
1	cup milk
3	tablespoons all-purpose flour

In a deep bowl, combine eggs, milk, and flour. Set aside.

ASSEMBLY AND PRESENTATION

all-purpose flour
1   *head iceberg lettuce, sliced*
    fresh parsley sprigs

Fill each avocado half with meat, pressing firmly to secure. Using 2 spoons, coat the filled halves with egg batter and then roll lightly in flour. Using a French-fry basket or a slotted spoon, fry one at a time in hot oil (350 to 375 degrees) a few minutes or until golden brown.

To serve, place one fried avocado half on a bed of lettuce and drizzle with sauce. Garnish with a sprig of fresh parsley.

STORAGE, FREEZING, AND ADVANCE PREPARATION

The sauce may be prepared in advance and refrigerated 2 to 3 days or frozen. The avocados may be prepared 6 to 8 hours ahead, coated with lemon juice, and stuffed. Refrigerate until ready to coat with batter and flour and deep-fry.

SHRIMP IN SALSA DIABLA

Be sure to see the recipe for Mario's Shrimp in Garlic Sauce (p. 190). It has the oil he uses for sautéing the shrimp in this recipe.

¼   *yellow onion, chopped*
2   *cloves garlic, peeled and minced*
1—2 *tablespoons vegetable oil*

Sauté the onion and garlic in hot oil until soft and translucent.

2   *tomatoes, cores intact*
3—4 *chiles de árboles* or *small hot chiles such as japones, stemmed and seeded*
3—4 *cilantro sprigs*
¼   *teaspoon salt*
¼   *teaspoon white pepper*

Meanwhile, place the tomatoes on a lightly oiled cookie sheet 4 inches from the broiling element. Leave the oven door ajar and turn the tomatoes to roast all sides. The skins will split. During the last few minutes, reduce the heat, add the chiles, and roast briefly about 2 minutes.

Transfer tomatoes, chiles, and all juices to a blender and puree along with cilantro, the garlic and onion mixture, and salt and pepper.

1   *cup chicken stock*
     salt to taste

Return to a medium-size skillet and simmer with chicken stock for 15 to 20 minutes to thicken. Adjust salt to taste and then keep warm while preparing the shrimp. The sauce is somewhat thin; if you simmer it 15 to 20 minutes, it will thicken.

2—2½ *pounds fresh medium-size shrimp*
2—4 *tablespoons garlic oil (see p. 190)*

Peel, devein, and butterfly the shrimp, leaving the tails intact. In a large skillet, heat about 2 tablespoons garlic oil and then sauté the shrimp for about 5 minutes. Turn over very briefly and then remove. Add more oil and sauté the remaining shrimp.

PRESENTATION

Spoon the sauce onto serving plates, placing the shrimp in the center. Serve with a fresh salad, preferably with fruit, and accompany the dish with French bread or flour tortillas.

STORAGE, FREEZING, AND ADVANCE PREPARATION

The sauce may be made a day or two ahead; however, shellfish are always best when served immediately after cooking.

CAPPY'S SCALLOPS
IN CHILE CREAM SAUCE
CAPPY'S SCALLOPS EN CASCABEL

This innovative dish from Cappy's is delicious when made with dried red chile pulp in the sauce or with poblano chile strips.

6 cascabel chiles or 4 dried California chiles or chiles anchos 1 quart water	Roast the chiles in a preheated 300-degree oven for 5 minutes. Stem and seed. Bring the water to a boil over medium heat. Add chiles and boil 20 to 25 minutes or until skin loosens. Remove from heat and let cool, covered, for 15 minutes. When cool enough to handle, discard peel, reserving all the pulp.
1 cup heavy cream 2 teaspoons cornstarch ¼ cup dry vermouth 1 tablespoon fresh lime juice 1 teaspoon sugar or to taste	In a blender, combine chile pulp with cream, cornstarch, vermouth, lime juice, and sugar and process until smooth. Set aside.
3 shallots, minced 1 bunch green onions, sliced 3 tablespoons butter 2 pounds sea scallops, large ones halved ½ pound snowpeas, ends trimmed	In a large skillet, sauté the shallots and green onions in butter 3 minutes. Add the scallops and cook, stirring constantly, until the scallops are barely firm, about 2 to 3 minutes. Add snowpeas, then stir in cream mixture and bring to a boil. Stir and continue cooking 2 to 3 minutes.
PRESENTATION	Serve immediately in gratin dishes with French bread or flour tortillas.
VARIATION	This is also delicious served over white rice, fish pasta, or buttered and toasted French bread. You could use a combination of shrimp and scallops if desired.

AUTHOR'S NOTE

Cascabel chiles are difficult to obtain; however, the California or ancho chiles work very well. Simplify this dish by omitting the preparation for dried chiles and using instead 6 poblano chiles. Roast and peel them as on page 27, then cut them into strips. Sauté the strips with the shallots and onions.

STORAGE, FREEZING, AND
ADVANCE PREPARATION

The chiles may be soaked and scraped early in the day; however, this dish is best when cooked just prior to serving. The snowpeas will stay brighter and the scallops are best when cooked to order; reheating fish almost always results in overcooking.

SHRIMP AND CRABMEAT CREPES VERACRUZANAS

This is a perfect example of Ernesto's masterful blending of classic ingredients in his own unique and innovative way. The results became one of his most popular new dishes.

THE CREPES

1¾   cups flour
¾   cup milk
¾   cup water
4   eggs
1   teaspoon vanilla
½   stick butter, melted
      pinch of salt
      butter

Thoroughly mix or blend the flour, milk, water, eggs, vanilla, melted butter, and salt until smooth. Let the batter stand for 1 to 2 hours or refrigerate overnight.

To prepare the crepes, heat a dab of butter in a well-seasoned crepe pan. Pour about ¼ cup batter in the corner of the pan and then immediately tilt to cover the entire surface. When the top is no longer liquid, turn to lightly brown both sides. Be sure to place filling on the second side, leaving the attractive side visible.

Stack crepes and cover until ready to use.

THE SAUCE VERACRUZANA

4–5   scallions, sliced
1½   sticks butter, at room temperature
2   poblano chiles, roasted, peeled, and cut in ¼-by-1-inch strips
4   cilantro sprigs, minced
2   tomatoes, peeled, seeded, and chopped
10   green olives, sliced
1   tablespoon capers

In a medium-size skillet, sauté the scallions in 1 tablespoon butter 5 minutes or until soft. Add the chile strips, cilantro, tomatoes, olives, and capers. Lower the heat. Whisk in the rest of the soft butter about 1½ tablespoons at a time, lifting the pan from the heat if necessary to prevent the butter from bubbling. Continue whisking until the sauce is smooth and creamy. Place over hot water, off direct heat, until ready to serve.

THE FILLING

12	medium-size shrimp, peeled and deveined
7	ounces crabmeat
12	crisp white mushrooms, sliced
2	tablespoons butter

Reserve 6 whole shrimp for garnish and then coarsely chop the rest. Sauté crabmeat, shrimp, and mushrooms in butter for 3 to 4 minutes. Stir in 3–4 tablespoons sauce Veracruzana. Set aside.

ASSEMBLY AND PRESENTATION

2	ounces white Mexican cheese or Monterey jack cheese, grated
	reserved whole shrimp
	flour
½	tablespoon butter
½	tablespoon oil
	minced fresh parsley

Fill each crepe with 1–2 tablespoons of the sauce Veracruzana. Roll, folding the edges inward to encase the filling. Brush with sauce to prevent drying out. Top with grated cheese and bake in a preheated 350-degree oven until the cheese is melted, about 12 minutes. Meanwhile, dust the shrimp lightly with flour and sauté in hot butter, oil, and parsley about 2 minutes. Nap the crepes with warm sauce and garnish every 2 crepes with 1 whole shrimp.

STORAGE, FREEZING, AND ADVANCE PREPARATION

The crepes and filling may be prepared 12 hours in advance or prepared and frozen. The sauce will hold over hot water for 1 to 2 hours.

FLOUNDER VERACRUZANA

It was fascinating to find such a good fish entrée miles from the coast in an area isolated enough that obtaining fresh fish would be most difficult. I have included this simple, tasty recipe as it gives a foolproof way to serve fish when necessity dictates a frozen product.

2	8–9-ounce flounder filets juice of 2 lemons	Wash flounder filets and then squeeze the lemon juice over both sides. Do this ½ hour before baking. Do not marinate longer than ½ hour.
6 2 ¼	tablespoons butter cloves garlic, minced cup fresh parsley, minced	In a baking dish large enough to accommodate both filets, melt half the butter. Top with minced garlic and parsley and pour remaining melted butter on top. Bake at 375 degrees, covered, 10 to 12 minutes or until just done.
1 1 1 1 3 4 8	yellow onion, cut in thin strips bell pepper, cut in ¼-by-1-inch strips tablespoon butter tablespoon vegetable oil tomatoes, peeled and seeded, or 1 1-pound can Italian-style tomatoes, roughly chopped sweet salad peppers, chopped green olives, sliced	In a medium-size skillet, sauté onion and pepper strips until tender, using as much butter and oil as necessary. Stir in tomatoes, salad peppers, and olives, and bring to a boil. Simmer 3 to 4 minutes.

PRESENTATION

	cooked fresh green peas or minced fresh parsley	Serve topped with the sauce. You may garnish the dish with green peas or parsley.

AUTHOR'S NOTE

The salad peppers are sweet, not hot; they are usually labeled as salad peppers. Italian-style tomatoes can be found in most supermarkets.

STORAGE, FREEZING, AND
ADVANCE PREPARATION

The sauce may be made a day ahead and reheated. Carmela uses frozen fish, which was very good; red snapper may also be used. I suggest soaking the fish 5 to 10 minutes in salted milk before baking.

FISH IN GARLIC SAUCE
PESCADO AL MOJO DE AJO

The sauce for this dish is like a French *beurre blanc*—opaque and creamy. Follow the instructions carefully to avoid overheating the butter and causing it to look clear or separate. Mike leaves the garlic bits moderately coarse.

THE BUTTER SAUCE

1	*clove garlic*
1½	*sticks butter, at room temperature*

Heat the garlic with 1 tablespoon butter; do not allow the butter to bubble. Over very low heat, whisk in additional soft butter, about 1 tablespoon at a time, to make a smooth and creamy sauce. Lift the pan from the heat if necessary to avoid separating the sauce. Strain and then keep warm, off direct heat, so the sauce doesn't separate.

THE GARLIC BITS

1–2	*tablespoons vegetable oil*
4	*large cloves garlic, coarsely chopped*

In a small frying pan, heat the vegetable oil and sauté the garlic bits 5 to 8 minutes or until very lightly browned. Drain garlic bits on paper towels.

THE FISH

4	*red snapper* or *swordfish filets (approximately 8 ounces each) fresh lemon juice vegetable oil*

Clean fish filets and then squeeze lemon juice over each one. Brush both sides with vegetable oil. Broil fish with skin side down about 3 minutes. Turn and brush with garlic butter sauce; broil another 3 to 4 minutes until done.

PRESENTATION

	reserved garlic bits
¼	*cup fresh parsley, minced*

Transfer fish to a serving platter and garnish with garlic bits and minced parsley. A goodly amount of fresh parsley complements (and tempers) the garlic.

VARIATION

I prefer to begin the butter sauce with ¼ cup each vinegar and white wine, which I simmer with 1 minced shallot for 3 to 4 minutes.

STORAGE, FREEZING, AND ADVANCE PREPARATION

The butter sauce may be made 1 hour in advance and held over hot water or in a crockpot. However, for best results, prepare the fish just prior to serving.

MARINERO FISH

This specialty has been a favorite at both Mario's and Alberto's and Chiquita's for several years. It is worth the time involved in preparation. We found no loss of quality when substituting clam juice and water for fish stock, though watch the salt, as clam juice tends to be salty.

3–4	*fish heads and bones*	Crush 3–4 fish heads and then cover heads, bones, and other ingredients with water. Bring to a boil and then reduce the heat and boil gently for 8 to 10 minutes. Strain and set aside 3 cups for the sauce preparation. Freeze the remainder for another use.
1	*onion slice*	
	several cilantro sprigs	
1	*clove garlic, peeled*	
1	*teaspoon salt (omit if using clam juice)*	
1–1½	*quarts, more or less, water*	

OR   OR

2	*cups clam juice*	Bring the clam juice and water to a boil. Skim the foam that rises to the top and discard. Reserve the broth.
1	*cup water*	

6	*5–6-ounce fish filets, preferably* *flounder* or *red snapper* *juice of 2 limes*	Clean the filets. Squeeze lime juice over them and set aside.

2	*cloves garlic, minced*	In a 3-quart saucepan, combine fish stock (or clam juice mixture) with garlic, lemon juice, pepper, butter, olives, and shrimp. Bring to a boil and then reduce heat and simmer 10 to 15 minutes. Add the cheese in several batches, stirring until melted. Remove about ½ cup and dissolve the cornstarch in this liquid. Stir back into the sauce until thick and smooth. Set aside or refrigerate until ready to reheat and finish the dish.
3	*tablespoons fresh lemon juice*	
¼	*teaspoon white pepper*	
½	*stick butter*	
4	*green olives, chopped*	
8	*small shrimp, finely chopped*	
½	*pound Velveeta cheese, cut in small pieces*	
1½	*tablespoons cornstarch*	

1½	*pounds fresh spinach, stemmed* *and chopped*	Sauté the spinach in a large skillet with salt, garlic, and hot oil until tender and moisture has evaporated, about 3 to 4 minutes. Divide the spinach among the filets and then roll up to enclose the filling. Secure with a toothpick if desired.
1–2	*teaspoons salt*	
1	*clove garlic, minced*	
3–4	*tablespoons safflower oil*	

2   *tablespoons butter, melted*   Brush the filets with melted butter. Bake in buttered warm ramekins 8 to 10 minutes at 350 degrees. Reheat the cheese sauce over medium heat while the filets are baking.

PRESENTATION   Nap with warm cheese sauce just prior to serving.

STORAGE, FREEZING, AND ADVANCE PREPARATION   The sauce may be made ahead and refrigerated for 24 hours. The filets may be prepared for baking earlier in the day. Bring them to room temperature before baking or the cooking time will be adversely affected because of the chilled dishes. Cover with buttered wrap during refrigeration to prevent drying out.

STUFFED SNAPPER

7	ounces lump crabmeat
2	tablespoons butter

Sauté the crabmeat in butter 2 to 3 minutes. Set aside.

2	snapper filets (7 ounces each)
	fresh lime juice
	flour
	salt and pepper
	butter

Clean the fish and squeeze lime juice over each filet. Halve the fish horizontally to make a cavity for the stuffing. Lightly flour the outside of each filet, and then stuff with crab mixture. Close, sprinkle with salt and pepper, shaking off excess.

Bake in a buttered pan in a preheated 400-degree oven about 10 minutes. Brush with butter several times during baking. (Cooking time varies with thickness of the fish. When checking for doneness, remember the flesh should be just opaque but still appear quite wet.)

4	cloves garlic, finely chopped
1½	sticks unsalted butter, at room temperature
1–2	tablespoons fresh parsley, minced

In a medium-size skillet, sauté the garlic in 1 tablespoon butter until soft, about 2 minutes. Whisk in the remaining soft butter, 1½ tablespoons at a time, over low heat. Do not allow the mixture to simmer, and continue whisking until smooth and creamy. Add minced parsley and set the sauce aside over a pan of hot water to keep warm.

ASSEMBLY AND PRESENTATION

2	tomatoes
	butter

Remove the core and top portion from the tomatoes and then brush with butter. Broil 6 inches from the element for 5 to 8 minutes. Nap with part of the garlic butter sauce and keep warm.

minced fresh parsley
⅓ *cup toasted almonds* or *pine nuts*
2 *cups cooked white rice*

Nap each filet with garlic butter sauce and then garnish with parsley and toasted nuts. Serve over rice.

VARIATION

This is also good with the Veracruzana butter sauce used on Ernesto's crepes (see p. 180).

STORAGE, FREEZING, AND ADVANCE PREPARATION

The sauce may be prepared 1 to 2 hours in advance; however, the fish should be prepared just prior to serving.

MARIO'S SHRIMP IN GARLIC SAUCE

This is a recipe for garlic lovers. The crisp garlic bits are the secret . . . follow the instructions to the letter to avoid burning the garlic and spoiling the taste. The flavorful garlic oil that remains should be stored in the refrigerator and used for sautéing shrimp or any other meat or fowl.

12 *cloves garlic, roughly chopped* 1 *cup vegetable oil* ½ *stick unsalted butter, cut in 4 pieces*	In a large skillet, sauté the garlic in medium-hot oil (about 300 degrees) until light brown. Watch carefully so as not to burn. After about 6 to 8 minutes, quickly whisk in the butter and remove immediately from the fire. When all the butter has been added, the bits will become crisp. Remove them with a slotted spoon and reserve the oil and butter for sautéing the shrimp. Note: this same oil is used with Shrimp in Salsa Diabla (see p. 176).
1½ *pounds fresh medium-size shrimp, peeled, deveined, and butterflied (leave tails intact)* *salt to taste*	In a large skillet, heat about 2–3 tablespoons of the reserved oil and then sauté the shrimp for about 5 minutes. Turn over very briefly and then remove. Add more oil as necessary to sauté all the shrimp. Salt to taste.

PRESENTATION

minced fresh parsley *Mexican Rice (see p. 126)*	Garnish with the garlic bits and parsley. Serve with Mexican Rice.

VARIATION

I like to brush the garlic oil over French bread, then sprinkle it with parsley and toast it. Serve this with the shrimp and accompany the dish with a lettuce-and-tomato salad.

STORAGE, FREEZING, AND ADVANCE PREPARATION

The garlic bits may be prepared at least a day in advance, then toasted briefly under the broiler to crisp. The oil is then ready to use as desired.

GRILLING

To most Texans, there's no mystery or special knowledge when it comes to grilling—it's almost inborn. Texans have been cooking meals over live fires for centuries. All it takes is a good hot fire and a steak. Skirt steaks (fajitas) or T-bones or any well-marbled steaks are relatively easy to cook, as the heat is not critical (even a moderately low fire will sear the steak) and the fat content prevents the meat from drying out. Marinades are used both to add flavor and to tenderize tougher cuts of meat.

Grilling chicken, fish, or shellfish is another story. There are three problems: the absence of fat, loss of heat during longer cooking times, and the more critical temperature. Restaurateurs have an added problem home cooks avoid. Rather than having the luxury of cooking one meal when the fire reaches the perfect temperature, they are faced with hundreds of meals and mixed orders. Cooking meat, fish, and poultry on the same grill, when all require different temperatures, takes some expertise. Over the course of several hours, the fire will change constantly, adding to the frustration of an already stressful situation. Many grills have elaborate systems to raise and lower the grid surface, thus regulating the distance from the fire or enabling the fire to be rebuilt; however, customers are not often willing to wait while the grill temperature stabilizes.

The popularity of fajitas and grilled fish has increased the demand for mesquite grilling. Presentations vary and are outlined in this section. I visited over a hundred restaurants that specialize in mesquite grilling, in both Texas and California, and the inconsistencies in both the grills and the results were astounding. Everyone has a theory on marinades, wood versus mesquite charcoal (or a mixture of the two), and how to balance the different products over the same grill. Clearly, the expert in this area is Lawton Haygood of Turtle Cove in Dallas. While his specialty is seafood, he also serves steaks, poultry, wild game, and vegetables. A perfectionist when it comes to a fine-quality product, for several years Lawton has been working on a grill which solves the problems of inconsistent heat distribution, rapid burn of both charcoal and wood, and a cooking surface suitable for low-fat items such as poultry and fish without relying on oil to keep them from drying out. After watching him grill 350 dinners on a busy evening, all requiring precise cooking times, and then tasting the exquisite results, I was convinced. His grill and his expertise have revolutionized grilling.

Jesse Calvillo of La Fogata and Clive Duval of Tila's use a different grill but are also masters at their craft. They have contributed their favorite marinades and their secrets for grilling steaks, seafood, and poultry. These will serve the home cook well, as she or he does not have the problem of consistency on a volume basis.

Whether you grill over charcoal, mesquite charcoal, mesquite wood, or a combination of these, these tips should help you produce a delicious meal.

GRILLING TECHNIQUES

JESSE CALVILLO (Skirt Steaks, Chicken)

Marinade: For flavor, lemon or lime juice, Worcestershire sauce, black pepper
Peanut oil for brushing the meat

1. Marinate the meat at least 2 hours or, preferably, overnight.

2. Allow the fire to burn at least 15 minutes, both to reach the proper temperature and to eliminate charcoal taste.

3. Cook fajitas quickly, over a hot, open flame. Turn 2 to 3 times, brushing with peanut oil to encourage a live flame. This renders the fat from the meat and gives it a good flavor.

4. Grill the chicken over a cooler portion of the grill or with a fire that has burned down to a cooler temperature. Cook slowly, with the skin on, brushing with oil, for about 7 minutes on each side. Cooking time may vary with the weight and thickness of the meat.

5. Meats may be grilled in advance, taking care not to overcook. Remove them from the grill when the juices still run red, then wrap securely in foil to keep moist and warm. The meat will continue to cook; therefore, it is important to remove it from the fire before it becomes well done or dries out.

6. Jesse, consistent with his peers, recommends buying "inside skirt steaks." Thick ones should be butterflied before marinating and trimmed of excess fat.

Presentation for skirt steaks or fajitas:

San Antonio Fiesta Fajitas: Cut the cooked meat into small individual portions that will fit in a flour tortilla. Serve with pico de gallo and sliced avocados.

San Antonio Sizzling Fajitas: Cut the meat in strips and then serve on a heated platter. Accompany with guacamole in a *molcajete* (mortar and pestle), fresh tomato salsa, and fresh flour tortillas.

Tacos al Carbón: Cut the meat in bite-size pieces and then serve in a soft flour tortilla with avocado slices and pico de gallo. Jesse sometimes adds beans or cheeses.

Taco Norteño: A La Fogata variation of Tacos al Carbón where the tortilla is filled with beans, cheese, avocado, and salsa and then grilled until semicrisp.

Carne Asada or Carne Tampiqueña: Whole skirt steaks, in a strip about 1/3 to 1/4 the total steak, served with guacamole and an enchilada.

Tila's Fajitas: Chunks of chicken or skirt steak, grilled and then marinated in a warm tomato, onion, and chile salsa. Served in flour tortillas.

Dallas Fajitas: Strips of skirt steak or chicken, served San Antonio–style on a sizzling platter, with fresh lime juice squeezed over them before serving. Standard accompaniments of flour tortillas, salsa, and guacamole in a *molcajete*.

LAWTON HAYGOOD (Fish, Chicken, Steaks, Game)

Mesquite wood

Marinade: Occasionally, for poultry or game, with fresh herbs and spices to complement the meat, for flavor. In most cases, marinades are not necessary.

Melted margarine for seasoning the grill or brushing red snapper and poultry

1. Use only seasoned (aged at least 1 year) mesquite wood. Green wood will produce an unpleasant, strong smoke and a bitter flavor.

2. Build your fire, if possible, 6 to 8 inches from the product. Allow the fire to burn down and stabilize. This will help insure a constant heat to give the moist, desired result in all meats or poultry.

3. Brush the grill surface with melted margarine prior to placing the meat or fish on it. This helps prevent the fish from sticking. A nonstick vegetable coating spray is also helpful and should be applied before starting the fire, then reapplied when the fire stabilizes. (If the heat source is 4 inches from the grill surface, this may not apply.) When turning the fish, use the same coating spray on the spatula.

4. Judge the temperature in the following way. Hold your hand over the grill and count to 5 for steaks, 10 for fish or poultry. The temperature for fish is more critical than that for beef; do not allow flames or sparks to blacken the fish. If marinating with oil, be sure to drain well as dripping oil causes a flame which may cause the fish to taste bitter.

5. Place the fish with the head toward you. When turned with a seasoned, long spatula in this manner, the flesh is less likely to tear.

6. Consistently check the temperature, particularly when adding fresh wood. Use the same 5 or 10 method. For swordfish, shrimp, and salmon: Cook at the same temperature—moderately hot. For red snapper and redfish: Cook at a moderate temperature.

NOTE	*Though you will have slightly better flavor, it is not essential to grill shrimp with the shell on. Use wood skewers to prevent shrimp from falling through the grill.*

7. Always remove fish just before it is completely cooked, as it continues to cook when removed. Overcooked fish will taste bitter or strong. The fish should be turned just as it looks opaque. Experience will tell you when.

8. When the grill surface is the proper distance from the heat and the heat source stable so you can best utilize the cooking surface, it is not necessary to oil the fish. Lawton believes the moist heat from mesquite wood, when properly used, will give a perfect, moist, and flavorful result without oils or marinades.

PRESENTATION FOR STEAKS, FISH, AND POULTRY	Butter sauce with lemon and mesquite-grilled vegetable assortment, fresh pasta or new potatoes.

CLIVE DUVAL (Fish, Chicken, Steaks)

Mesquite charcoal
Marinade: For flavor or to tenderize the inside skirt.

1. Clive prefers the flavor from mesquite charcoal, made from the large mesquite trees in Mexico. He uses a grill designed in California, which is much the same as that used in California restaurants.

2. In Clive's experience, lime should be used for flavor during or after grilling, not as a marinade unless accompanied with sufficient oil. Otherwise, the meat fibers may toughen unless tenderized. He prefers the less fatty inside skirt steak, which is butterflied.

3. Do not use salt in marinades or when grilling. It draws out the natural juices. Marinades should be oil-based with fresh herbs for flavor. Equally good results may be obtained with a 5-to-10-minute marinade of wine and citrus juices.

4. Allow the fire to burn down and stabilize so the sparks die down.

5. Take care not to overcook, particularly when using mesquite charcoal. The product will continue to cook when removed from the grill.

6. Grill chicken with the skin on, using moderate heat. When dicing for chicken fajitas, you may remove the skin when cutting, after grilling.

7. When grilling vegetables, blanch before grilling for 30 to 45 seconds. Season with cayenne, paprika, or salt and pepper and brush lightly with safflower oil.

8. When grilling white onions, prebake, dipped first in lemon juice, pepper, and safflower oil, for 5 to 8 minutes or until tender-crisp, then finish quickly on the grill for flavor.

9. Both chicken and skirt steaks for fajitas may be grilled in advance, removed when slightly undercooked, and then held in a sauté of tomatoes, jalapeños, onions, pepper, and a touch of safflower oil. The meats will stay juicy and tender for 3 to 4 hours.

PRESENTATION

Grilled swordfish, redfish, and shrimp with grilled vegetables; grilled skirt steaks with grilled onions; chicken and skirt steak fajitas in flour tortillas.

AUTHOR'S TIP

When preparing grilled vegetables for volume entertaining, grill the vegetables to mark them, then transfer to a cookie sheet, cover with foil, and keep warm in a slow oven. You may add seasonings and brush lightly with butter and lime juice if desired.

YIELD: About 5 cups or enough for 1 skirt steak
(2½ pounds, more or less)

MARINADE FOR FLANK STEAKS AND SKIRT STEAKS

Clive recommends never using salt, as it toughens the meat. Salt the meat after grilling, or suggest that people salt their own at the table.

2   bottles Corona Beer
2   cups safflower oil
5   jalapeño chiles, stemmed and chopped
5   cloves garlic, minced
2   tablespoons black pepper
¼   cup soy sauce
3–4 cilantro sprigs, minced

Blend all the ingredients and place in a shallow glass dish, about 10 by 11 by 2 inches deep. Be sure to rub the marinade into the meat and turn it several times during the marinating time.

AUTHOR'S NOTE

Marinate skirt steaks 12 hours or overnight. Flank steak needs no more than 3 to 4 hours. (The red wine vinegar acts faster on the better cut of meat.) Be sure to rub the marinade into the meat.

MARINADE FOR SPIT-ROASTED CHICKENS

Clive Duval marinates chickens 12 hours before grilling. His secrets are as follows: (1) marinate as directed, (2) cook chickens slowly, over low heat, (3) enjoy the fact that the fat drips out and sizzles perfectly. Basting is not necessary.

3	jalapeño chiles, seeded and chopped	Blend the chopped jalapeños with the garlic, cilantro, oil, wine, and juices. Whisk thoroughly to blend ingredients. Rub the chickens with a little of the marinade and fresh-ground black pepper. Marinate at least 12 hours before grilling.
3	cloves garlic, minced	
1/2	bunch cilantro, minced	
2	cups safflower oil	
2/3	cup white wine	
2/3	cup fresh lime juice	
2/3	cup fresh orange juice	
	fresh-ground black pepper	

NINFA'S MARINADE

Grilled meats and seafood are Ninfa Laurenzo's specialty—and one recipe has created her reputation. This marinade doubles as a glaze which may be used to brush the items during grilling.

1	*stick butter* or *margarine*
¼	*teaspoon garlic powder*
	juice of 1 lemon
	salt and pepper to taste
1	*tablespoon cooking sherry*
3	*tablespoons teriyaki sauce*

In a skillet or sauté pan, melt the butter. Stir in the garlic powder, lemon juice, salt and pepper, sherry, and teriyaki sauce. Simmer 2 to 3 minutes, stirring constantly to blend ingredients.

GRILLED SHRIMP

I like to serve these with Ernesto's Hot Sauce (see p. 41) or Mario's Salsa Diabla (see p. 176).

1½–2 pounds medium-size shrimp

juice of 2 limes
½   cup peanut oil
3   cloves garlic, minced
2–3 cilantro leaves

Peel and devein the shrimp, leaving the tails intact.

Combine the marinade ingredients and then marinate the shrimp, covered, for at least ½ to 2 hours.

Prepare the grill, making a medium-hot fire. Have the grill surface about 3 to 4 inches from the coals. You may wish to skewer the shrimp to prevent them from falling between the grids. Place shrimp atop the grill. Grill 1½ minutes, then turn, brush lightly with marinade, and grill an additional 1 to 1½ minutes. (Large shrimp will take 2 to 2½ minutes longer.)

Serve with the sauce of your choice.

GRILLED SWORDFISH

Swordfish is grilled quickly over a hot fire or flat top. Serve with black beans, grated Muenster or feta cheese, Mexican rice, and salad.

6	fresh swordfish steaks, 1 inch thick (6–8 ounces each)
2	cloves garlic, minced
	fresh-ground black pepper

Rub the swordfish steaks with garlic and black pepper.

½	cup white wine
1	cup chicken stock
½	cup safflower oil
¼	cup onion, minced
2–3	celery leaves
1	tablespoon hot red chile pepper flakes

Whisk or blend all ingredients together. Place the swordfish in the marinade and rub both marinade and seasonings into the fish. Let marinate for 2 hours.

Prepare the grill, making a medium-hot fire. Brush swordfish with oil and then grill 2 to 3 minutes per side. Brush each side with the marinade during the cooking time. Remember the steaks will continue to cook after removal from the grill.

If using a griddle or skillet, sauté over medium-high heat in clarified butter or half butter, half oil, for 2 to 3 minutes per side. Fish should be barely opaque, never dry, when done.

Desserts

MARIO'S AND ALBERTO'S
Top to Bottom: Marinero Fish with Beet
and Orange Garnish
Mexican Hot Sauce

Mario's Shrimp in Garlic Sauce
Far Right: Sopaipillas with Coconut Ice
Cream and Fresh Raspberries
Far Left: Sopaipillas with Cinnamon.

DESSERTS

Cajeta Crepes	Ernesto's
Sopaipillas	La Hacienda
Capirotada	Author's Contribution
Mariano's Fruitcake	Mariano's
Dessert Cobblers	The Tavern
Almond Flan	Fonda San Miguel
Praline Dessert	La Esquina
Banana Capitán	Las Canarias
Coffee Toffee Pie	Fonda San Miguel
Mango Ice Cream	Bennie Ferrell Catering
Pineapple and Oranges Tequila	Author's Contribution
Buñuelos	Las Canarias
Mexican Nut Cookies	Author's Contribution

CAJETA CREPES

The cajeta sauce is made fresh by Ernesto for his crepes (see p. 180). You may use a prepared sauce; however, your result will be more like a caramel sauce. Simply mix with cream and brandy to a pourable consistency.

2	quarts whole milk
3	cups sugar
¾	teaspoon baking soda

In a large stockpot, stir together the milk, sugar, and baking soda to dissolve the sugar. Then bring to a boil over medium-high heat. Simmer, stirring occasionally, for 4 to 5 hours or until very thick and caramel in color. Refrigerate until ready to use.

| 1½ | cups pecans, chopped |
| 2 | tablespoons butter |

Sauté the pecans in butter and then place in a 350-degree oven and toast until crisp, about 8 minutes. Set aside.

ASSEMBLY AND PRESENTATION

| 2 | ounces brandy |
| 8 | crepes (see p. 180) |

When ready to serve, reheat about 1½ cups of the sauce in a 12-to-14-inch skillet along with the pecans and brandy. When the sauce simmers, add 1 crepe at a time, using tongs or 2 forks to fold into a triangular shape. When all are folded, remove from heat and transfer to serving dishes. Spoon additional sauce over each serving, and garnish with pecans.

STORAGE, FREEZING, AND ADVANCE PREPARATION

The sauce may be made 2 days ahead and refrigerated until ready to use.

SOPAIPILLAS

These delicious puffs of pastry may be served with meals or dipped into confectioner's sugar and served for dessert with honey or fruit butters. Be sure to note the technique of spooning hot oil over the sopaipillas as they fry. This insures that they will puff and be light.

1	cup all-purpose bleached flour
2	teaspoons baking powder
1	teaspoon salt
1	tablespoon sugar
1	tablespoon vegetable shortening

Put the flour, baking powder, salt, sugar, and shortening in a mixing bowl. Use your fingers or a pastry blender to thoroughly combine and evenly distribute shortening.

⅓	cup hot water
1–2	tablespoons flour, if needed

Add hot water and stir with a fork until mixture forms a dough. If dough is too dry to mold or knead, add a bit more water. If dough seems too wet, add 1–2 tablespoons flour. Knead a couple of times, then place in a plastic bag and let rise 1 hour in a warm place.

Lightly flour a work surface and roll dough into a rectangle about ⅛ to ¼ inch thick. If the dough seems too elastic to roll easily, cover and let rest a few minutes more, then roll again. Fold the dough in half and roll the rectangle again. Cut the dough into 3-by-4-inch rectangles.

peanut oil for frying
powdered sugar
honey

Heat at least 5 inches of oil in a 3-quart saucepan or deep-fryer to 350 to 360 degrees. Fry 1 or 2 at a time, spooning hot oil over the top to encourage puffing. Drain on paper towels. Immediately dust with powdered sugar and serve with honey.

AUTHOR'S NOTE

I like to serve these with homemade fruit butters. The orange mango butter is one of my favorites.

ORANGE MANGO BUTTER

	zest from 1 orange
8	ounces cream cheese
1½	sticks unsalted butter
6–8	tablespoons powdered sugar
1	fresh mango or papaya, diced

Thoroughly cream the zest, cream cheese, butter, and powdered sugar. Blend in diced fruit. You may substitute ½ can mango, well drained, for the fresh.

HONEY PINEAPPLE BUTTER

	zest from 1 orange
½	cup fresh pineapple, pureed
1½	cups creamy honey
1½	sticks unsalted butter
½	teaspoon vanilla
4–6	tablespoons powdered sugar

Thoroughly cream all the ingredients to make a smooth butter. Adjust the amount of sugar to personal taste.

STORAGE, FREEZING, AND ADVANCE PREPARATION

Sopaipillas may be made several hours ahead but should be fried just prior to serving. The butters may be made 2 hours in advance.

CAPIROTADA

Many bread puddings are made with a sugar syrup in place of cream. This is my adaptation of an authentic recipe which has a cream and sugar syrup. Rich but outstanding.

⅔ cup almonds or *pecans, coarsely chopped*	Combine nuts, apples, and raisins. Set aside.
2–3 apples, peeled, cored, and coarsely chopped	
½ cup golden seedless raisins	

¾ cup brown sugar, *firmly packed*	In a medium-size saucepan, combine sugar, water, sherry, if desired, cinnamon sticks, clove, and anise seeds and bring to a boil over medium-high heat. Let boil 2 minutes. Strain and set aside. When cool, whip in egg yolks and cream.
½ cup water	
2 tablespoons sherry (optional)	
2 sticks cinnamon	
1 whole clove	
1 teaspoon anise seeds	
2 egg yolks, beaten	
1 cup heavy cream	

5 day-old sweet Mexican breads or *rolls or 9 ½-inch-thick slices stale French bread, crusts trimmed*	Preheat oven to 350 degrees. Butter a 1½-quart casserole (at least 3 inches deep) or soufflé dish. Trim thin portion of top and bottom crusts from the Mexican pastry, if using. Cut it into ½-inch-thick slices. Melt about 5 tablespoons butter in a large skillet over medium-high heat. Add pan dulce or bread slices in batches and sauté on both sides until golden, about 2 minutes, adding more butter if necessary. Remove from skillet. Melt the remaining butter.
1½ sticks butter	

4 ounces queso fresco or *cream cheese, chilled and crumbled*	Arrange 3 slices in bottom of prepared dish. Cover with ⅓ of the nut filling. Sprinkle with ⅓ of the cheese, then drizzle with ⅓ of the syrup. Repeat layering twice, alternating slices to cover empty spaces. Pour remaining melted butter over top. Press down gently on slices to soak well.

AUTHOR'S CONTRIBUTION

2   egg whites, at room temperature
¼   cup almonds or pecans
3   tablespoons brown sugar, firmly
        packed
1   teaspoon cinnamon

Beat egg whites in a large bowl until stiff but not dry. Combine nuts, sugar, and cinnamon. Gently fold sugar mixture into whites. Spread the topping over the pudding. Bake 35 minutes. Turn oven off and let the pudding stand in oven 15 minutes before serving.

PRESENTATION

Serve with whipped cream, ice cream, or a custard sauce flavored with a brandy or fruit liqueur.

AUTHOR'S NOTE

The mild California goat cheeses are excellent in this recipe.

STORAGE, FREEZING, AND
ADVANCE PREPARATION

The entire pudding may be assembled and then refrigerated overnight. Return to room temperature before baking.

MARIANO'S FRUITCAKE

This is a prized recipe from Mariano's father, who is responsible for many of the delicious recipes in Mariano's restaurants. I have taken the liberty of substituting Mexican candied fruit for the standard candied fruit mix which somehow seems natural. The cake keeps moist for several months, particularly when soaked with the optional glaze. Miniloaves of this cake make an excellent gift.

½	*pound dark seedless raisins*
1	*pound candied pumpkin or candied papayas, cut in small pieces*
1	*pound dates, snipped*
½	*pound candied cherries*
¼	*pound candied citron, cut in small pieces*
½	*pound candied pineapple or candied oranges, diced*
¼	*pound candied sweet potatoes, cut in small pieces*
1	*pound pecans, walnuts, pine nuts, almonds, or any combination of nuts, chopped*
¼	*cup bourbon*

At least 2 hours ahead or overnight, soak the fruits and nuts in bourbon, stirring several times. Reserve several whole nuts for the garnish.

2	*sticks unsalted butter*
½	*pound brown sugar (about 1 cup + 3 tablespoons), loosely packed*
8	*eggs, separated*
2	*cups unbleached all-purpose flour*
½	*tablespoon cinnamon*
½	*tablespoon ground cloves*
½	*tablespoon allspice*
½	*tablespoon ground coriander or mace*
½	*tablespoon nutmeg*
½	*teaspoon salt*
¼	*cup red wine*
¼	*cup orange juice concentrate*

Butter an angel food cake or bundt pan and set aside.

In a large bowl, cream the butter with the brown sugar. Add the egg yolks, 2 at a time, beating after each addition.

Sift together the flour and spices. Add to the egg mixture along with the wine and orange juice concentrate.

In a separate bowl, beat the egg whites until stiff but not dry; then fold into the batter alternately with the fruits and nuts.

Transfer the batter to the prepared pan and bake in a preheated 250-degree oven for 3 hours. The extra batter may be baked in miniloaf pans along with the cake. Take them out 30 to 35 minutes before the large cake. Garnish with whole nuts.

OPTIONAL GLAZE

2	*medium-size oranges*
½	*cup granulated sugar*
6	*tablespoons butter*
⅓	*cup bourbon*

Using a stripper, remove peel from both oranges and set aside. Squeeze all the juice into a medium-size skillet along with the sugar, butter, and bourbon and bring to a boil. Add the strips of peel and simmer about 4 to 5 minutes. Cool 5 minutes; then spoon over warm cake, using a rack for the cake. Reserve the juice; then spoon over the cake again, repeating the procedure until all the glaze is absorbed. Wrap the cake in a damp towel and remoisten every few days.

STORAGE, FREEZING, AND ADVANCE PREPARATION

The fruits and nuts may be prepared a day ahead. I usually do this in addition to measuring all the ingredients. The cake is best made several weeks prior to serving. I like to glaze the cake, then wrap it for seasoning for about 4 weeks. It is delicious served within 1 or 2 days but slices better after 3 days.

DESSERT COBBLERS

Carmela López' method of preparing the fruit and pastry separately makes an especially flaky, light, and delicious cobbler. This makes the fruit easy to heat without overbaking the crust, for it and the pastry will be combined at serving.

4	*pints fresh strawberries, blueberries,* or *other seasonal berries* or *12–14 fresh peaches* or *8 papayas* or *2 fresh pineapples*
1	*cup sugar*
1	*cup water*
2	*tablespoons cornstarch*
2	*tablespoons fresh lemon juice food coloring for berries (optional)*

Wash and hull berries. If using fresh whole fruit, peel, core, and cut into bite-size pieces. Use about ⅓ the total amount of fruit to make the sauce. Set the remaining fruit aside.

In a blender, puree the ⅓ portion of fruit with sugar and half the water. Stir together the cornstarch, lemon juice, and food coloring, if desired. Combine with remaining water and cook in a 1-quart saucepan over medium heat until thick and clear, about 5 minutes. Cool 10 minutes. Add reserved fruit and taste to adjust sugar. Refrigerate at least 2 hours.

10	*tablespoons vegetable shortening*
2	*cups all-purpose bleached flour*
2	*tablespoons sugar*
½	*teaspoon salt*
1	*tablespoon vinegar*
1	*teaspoon vanilla*
6–8	*tablespoons ice water*
1	*tablespoon cinnamon sugar*

Using a pastry blender (or your food processor with a metal blade), combine the shortening with flour, sugar, and salt to make a coarse, crumbly mixture. Add the vinegar and vanilla, and then pulse in enough ice water to make a pastry dough. The pastry should hold together but not feel extremely wet.

Let the dough rest 20 minutes, re-frigerated and covered with waxed paper, and then roll out onto a lightly floured surface into a rectangle about ¼ inch thick. Transfer to a cookie sheet or jelly roll pan. Prick in several places and then sprinkle with cinnamon sugar. Bake in a preheated 375-degree oven until lightly browned, about 12 to 15 minutes. Cool, then store pastry at room temperature.

ASSEMBLY AND PRESENTATION

sweetened whipped cream or *ice cream*

When ready to serve, spoon a portion of the fruit into a dish. Heat in a microwave oven 15 to 20 seconds, if desired. Break the pastry into pieces and place atop the fruit. Top with sweetened whipped cream or ice cream.

AUTHOR'S NOTE

For a festive touch, try combining fruits, such as blueberries and peaches or pineapple and straw-berries. You may top with quartered and fried flour tortillas, dredged in cinnamon sugar, in place of pastry. The cobbler fruits also make a delicious sauce for ice cream.

STORAGE, FREEZING, AND ADVANCE PREPARATION

Both the pastry and the fruit may be prepared ahead. The fruit mixture will freeze successfully. The pastry will remain crisp and light at room temperature for several days.

ALMOND FLAN

The nuts form a crust when the flan is unmolded. If you prefer to omit the nuts, you need not change any other ingredients.

2	tablespoons water
½	cup granulated sugar

Stir water into sugar and then, using an 8-to-9-inch skillet, bring the mixture to a boil. Use a brush dipped in water to wash down any sugar crystals clinging to the sides of the pan. Continue to boil over high heat, undisturbed, until the mixture turns a rich amber color. Once it turns, you may stir. When it is golden brown (caramelized), remove from the heat. It may smell burned—caramelized sugar literally is burned sugar. Immediately pour the sugar into a 9-inch cake pan at least 3 inches deep so the sugar coats all sides, or use 8 individual custard cups, well buttered.

¾–1	cup slivered almonds or pine nuts, finely chopped
1	13½-ounce can evaporated milk
1	cup whole milk
1	teaspoon vanilla
3	eggs, beaten
3	egg yolks
¾	cup granulated sugar

Beat together the remaining ingredients. Pour into the prepared pan or cups. Then place in a larger pan, half filled with water. Cover with foil and bake for 55 minutes to 1 hour at 350 degrees, or until the custard is set.

Remove from oven, uncover, and cool out of the water at room temperature 30 minutes. Refrigerate, unmolded and covered, until ready to serve. The sauce will soften during refrigeration. Simply run a knife around the edge and invert to unmold.

VARIATION

You may use pumpkin for an interesting version of this recipe: 1 cup pureed cooked pumpkin, ⅓ cup additional sugar, and 1 teaspoon orange zest.

STORAGE, FREEZING, AND ADVANCE PREPARATION

The flan may be prepared 2 days in advance.

PRALINE DESSERT

If you are looking for a simple yet impressive dessert, try this combination from La Esquina. Use your favorite pralines and the best-quality ice cream, preferably homemade.

	oil for frying	In a saucepan, bring at least 3 inches of oil to 375 degrees and then, 3 or 4 at a time, fry the tortillas until crisp, browning both sides. This takes just under a minute. Immediately coat with cinnamon sugar.
6	*flour tortillas, quartered*	
	cinnamon sugar	

1½ quarts vanilla ice cream
10–12 firm pralines, broken

Let the ice cream soften enough to allow you to stir the broken pralines throughout it. Refreeze until firm.

½ cup cajeta sauce (see p. 205) or prepared caramel sauce
¼ cup heavy cream or half-and-half
¼ cup Kahlúa

Meanwhile, combine the cajeta or caramel sauce with cream or half-and-half and Kahlúa. Warm this mixture just prior to serving.

½–¾ cup whole or slightly broken pecans
2 tablespoons butter

Sauté the pecans in butter for several minutes and then drain on paper towels.

ASSEMBLY AND PRESENTATION

Arrange 4 of the buñuelo quarters in a serving dish. Place a scoop of ice cream on top, then drizzle with sauce. Top with pecans.

STORAGE, FREEZING, AND ADVANCE PREPARATION

The entire dessert may be prepared in advance and then assembled just prior to serving. I often prescoop the ice cream if serving a large crowd.

BANANA CAPITÁN

An attractive and very festive dessert. Freely substitute fruits according to the season. Purists may choose to prepare homemade flour tortillas to fry—a definite improvement.

peanut oil for frying
2   flour tortillas, quartered
    cinnamon sugar

Heat 2 to 3 inches of oil to 375 degrees in a small saucepan. Using tongs, fry the tortillas about 30 seconds or until crisp. Drain on paper towels and then coat with cinnamon sugar. Set aside.

4–5 fresh mangoes, peeled and sliced
½   cup fresh lime juice
½   cup sugar
¼   cup water
1–2 ounces Grand Marnier

In a medium-size saucepan, cook the mangoes with lime juice, sugar, and water for 10 to 15 minutes, stirring constantly to prevent burning. Add liqueur during final 2 to 3 minutes. Chill 2 to 3 hours; the sauce should be very cold.

ASSEMBLY AND PRESENTATION

4   bananas, halved lengthwise, then quartered
1   quart mango ice cream

To assemble, place banana pieces in a large stemmed goblet or brandy snifter. Add several scoops of mango ice cream and then spoon the sauce on top. Garnish with crisp tortilla quarters.

AUTHOR'S NOTE

When fresh mangoes are not available, substitute 1 16-ounce can mangoes, including juice, and reduce the sugar, adjusting the amount to taste. You may reduce the cooking time to 3 to 5 minutes. When raspberries or blueberries are in season, a few fresh berries are a colorful addition.

STORAGE, FREEZING, AND ADVANCE PREPARATION

The tortillas may be made a day ahead; however, the dessert should be assembled just prior to serving.

COFFEE TOFFEE PIE

When garnished with fresh strawberries, dipped in both white and dark chocolate, this creates a beautiful dessert.

THE CRUST

1	cup all-purpose flour
1	cup walnuts, chopped
1	ounce semisweet chocolate, ground
	dash of salt
1	stick cold butter, cut in 5–6 pieces
1	egg

Using a fork or pastry blender, combine the dry ingredients, cutting in the butter and the egg. Press into a 9-inch pie pan and let rest, refrigerated, 1 to 4 hours.

Prick in several places with a fork and bake at 375 degrees for 12 to 15 minutes or until brown. Cool.

THE FILLING

1	stick butter
3/4	cup brown sugar
1	ounce unsweetened chocolate, melted and cooled
2	teaspoons instant coffee
2	large eggs

Cream the butter and sugar together, then add cooled chocolate and instant coffee. Beat until smooth. Add the eggs 1 at a time. Pour into the cooled crust and refrigerate at least 2 hours until set.

ASSEMBLY AND PRESENTATION

1	cup whipping cream
2	tablespoons Kahlúa
1	tablespoon powdered sugar
	grated chocolate
	fresh strawberries (optional)

Whip the cream with the Kahlúa and powdered sugar. Mound atop pie and garnish with grated chocolate and fresh strawberries, if desired.

STORAGE, FREEZING, AND ADVANCE PREPARATION

After the filling is poured into the crust, the pie can be frozen and will keep indefinitely.

MANGO ICE CREAM

1   cup light cream
1   cup sweetened condensed milk
4   teaspoons vanilla
⅛   teaspoon salt

2   cups whipping cream
4   fresh mangoes, finely chopped
    (do not drain)

In a large mixing bowl, stir together light cream, condensed milk, vanilla, and salt.

Add whipping cream and then fold in mangoes with juice. Turn into an 8-by-8-by-2-inch pan or refrigerator tray. Cover and partially freeze. After about 2 hours, remove the mixture and break into chunks. In a blender or a food processor fitted with a metal blade, process the mixture until smooth. Return to a chilled 14-by-11-inch pan or refrigerator tray. Freeze until firm.

PINEAPPLE AND ORANGES TEQUILA

This simple, refreshing dessert is the perfect end to a spicy meal. The fruits may be marinated several days in advance. If you have time, the orange zest is a nice finishing touch.

2	ounces tequila
2	ounces triple-sec
1–2	tablespoons granulated sugar

Combine the marinade ingredients in a glass bowl.

1	fresh pineapple, peeled, halved, and cored
6	oranges

Slice the pineapple and set aside. Using a stripper, remove 12–14 strips of peel from the oranges and set aside. Then, using a sharp knife, cut away the remaining peel and membrane, exposing the orange flesh. Remove sections along the membrane, then squeeze all the juice from the pulp and reserve.

Place both pineapple slices and orange sections in the marinade and then add about ⅓ of the reserved orange juice. Refrigerate, covered, for 3 to 4 hours.

OPTIONAL GARNISH

strips of orange peel
reserved orange juice
2   *tablespoons granulated sugar*
granulated or *colored sugar*

Place strips of orange peel in reserved orange juice and sugar and bring to a boil. Boil for about 3 minutes, then remove and place on waxed paper which is lightly coated with sugar. Roll to coat and then set aside.

ASSEMBLY AND PRESENTATION

pineapple sherbet

When ready to serve, place fruit sections in each bowl. Top with a generous scoop of pineapple sherbet and drizzle juices over the top.

Garnish with orange zest, if desired, and quartered, fried flour tortillas dredged in cinnamon sugar.

BUÑUELOS

These buñuelos are unique because of the orange juice flavor and the quantity of eggs. Allowing the dough to rest is critical to achieving a satisfactory result. You may use these for the Banana Capitán (see p. 217) in place of the shorter version given in the recipe.

4   *cups all-purpose flour*
1   *teaspoon baking powder*
½   *teaspoon vanilla*
¼   *cup salad oil*
4   *eggs*
1¼   *cups fresh orange juice, slightly heated*

In a large bowl, stir together the flour, baking powder, vanilla, salad oil, and eggs. Then add warm orange juice and knead gently to combine all the ingredients. You may need to add a small amount of flour if the dough is extremely sticky. Let rest for 1 hour.

peanut oil for frying
cinnamon sugar

On a lightly floured surface, roll out the dough to ⅛ inch thickness. Cut rounds, strips, or any shape desired, and fry in deep fat at 375 degrees until crisp and golden brown. Drain on paper towels and then sprinkle with cinnamon sugar.

STORAGE, FREEZING, AND ADVANCE PREPARATION

Buñuelos may be fried in advance. They will keep for several days, as long as the initial frying produces a crisp result.

221

MEXICAN NUT COOKIES

These unusual cookies—hollow in the center—are a specialty in many Texas bakeries. They should be light in color, but crisp. Weighing the flour and powdered sugar is essential. I have used pine nuts in place of pecans.

1 cup pine nuts, finely chopped	Toast the nuts on a cookie sheet in a slow oven (275 degrees) for about 12 minutes. Do not brown. Set aside to cool.
6 tablespoons unsalted butter ¾ cup vegetable shortening ½ pound powdered sugar 1 teaspoon vanilla ½ teaspoon almond extract ½ pound cake flour ¼ teaspoon salt	Cream the butter, shortening, and sugar. Add the vanilla, almond extract, flour, salt, and nuts and mix to combine thoroughly.
powdered sugar or cinnamon sugar	Using your hands or a miniature ice cream scoop which has been sprayed with a nonstick vegetable coating, make rounds of dough on very lightly buttered cookie sheets. Bake at 350 degrees for about 12 to 15 minutes. Do not brown. Transfer to wire racks and sift a light coating of sugar over the cookies.
STORAGE, FREEZING, AND ADVANCE PREPARATION	The cookies keep very well, up to 2 weeks.

FROM MARIANO MARTÍNEZ

A dessert idea sure to please party guests. Halve a fresh papaya, leaving ¼ inch flesh with the skin intact. Fill the cavity with a lime, pineapple, or strawberry sorbet, then press halves together and refreeze. Peel off skin after 24 hours, and serve one half per person. Garnish with whipped cream and fresh mint.

Beverages

NINFA's
Top to Bottom:
Ham and Cheese
Seafood Cheese

Chihuahua Cheese
Center: Platter/Top and Bottom:
Grilled Shrimp with Ninfa's Marinade
Crab Enchiladas

BEVERAGES

Golden Mama

White Wine Sangría

Red Wine Sangría

Christmas Eve Punch

Cappy's

Ninfa's

Las Canarias

La Esquina

GOLDEN MAMA

Cappy's version of a margarita is outstanding.

3	ounces Cuervo Gold
1½	ounces Grand Marnier
4–5	ounces sweet-and-sour mix
2–3	tablespoons fresh orange juice
1	cup, more or less, shaved ice
	salt
2	limes, sliced

In a blender or highball shaker, vigorously combine the ingredients.

Turn a collins or highball glass into a bowl of salt to lightly coat rim, then fill with Golden Mama.

Twist each lime slice to make a wheel. Garnish and serve.

WHITE WINE SANGRÍA

This Sangría is quite sweet. If you prefer a less sweet version, use the full bottle of wine.

½   *cup fresh orange juice*
½   *cup pineapple juice*
¼   *cup water*
4   *tablespoons sugar*

In a small saucepan, bring fruit juices, water, and sugar to a boil. Set aside to cool.

11   *ounces white wine*
2   *ounces curaçao*
1   *ounce crème de banana*
1   *ounce brandy*
¼   *cup Sprite or 7-Up*

Add the cooked syrup to the wine, liqueurs, brandy, and Sprite or 7-Up. Mix well.

1   *lemon, thinly sliced and seeded*
1   *lime, thinly sliced and seeded*
2   *oranges, thinly sliced and seeded*
    thin slices of fresh pineapple and maraschino cherries (optional)

Serve in 4–6 ounce glasses and garnish with fresh lemon, lime, and orange slices. If desired, add a few pineapple slices and cherries.

STORAGE, FREEZING, AND ADVANCE PREPARATION

You may prepare this early in the day, but add the fruits just prior to serving.

RED WINE SANGRÍA

This traditional Sangría is a favorite beverage for Mexican specialties. The sweetness will vary according to the choice of red wine.

2   bottles red wine, preferably Bur-
     gundy, or a fruity wine
1   pint fresh orange juice
     juice of 6 lemons
1   pint ginger ale

In a large punch bowl, combine the wine, juices, and ginger ale.

2   lemons
4   limes
4   oranges

Thinly slice the lemons, limes, and oranges, and float in the Sangría prior to serving. Serve chilled over ice.

STORAGE, FREEZING, AND
ADVANCE PREPARATION

The Sangría may be prepared early in the day; however, add the fruit slices just prior to serving.

CHRISTMAS EVE PUNCH

Mr. and Mrs. Dino Nono of Dallas gave this traditional punch to the Anatole to serve in the lobby one Christmas season. Don't wait until Christmas to enjoy it!

3	*oranges*
½	*cup granulated sugar*

Using a stripper, remove long strips of peel from the oranges. Then bring all the strips and sugar to a boil in a skillet filled with enough water to cover. Simmer 8 to 10 minutes, then remove and reserve the peel.

20	*cups pineapple juice, heated*
¼	*pound white seedless raisins*
¼	*pound tamarind seeds*
10	*2-inch pieces raw sugarcane*
5	*guavas, quartered, or 2 cups guava nectar*
6	*ounces raw honey*
1	*stick cinnamon*
1	*cup brandy or to taste*
	orange zest
	cinnamon sticks (optional)

Slice the rest of the oranges and then bring all the ingredients to a simmer in a large stockpot. Let stand for 4 hours or overnight. If you cannot obtain sugarcane, you may use the syrup from the oranges, making up the remainder with ¼ cup brown sugar.

After 4 hours, strain the juice from all fruits and then discard fruits. Strain the punch and serve either hot or cold, garnished with the reserved orange strips and, if desired, cinnamon sticks.

STORAGE, FREEZING, AND ADVANCE PREPARATION

The punch may be made up to a week in advance.

INDEX